MY JOURNEY TO
SPIRITUAL
RESTORATION

MY JOURNEY TO
SPIRITUAL
RESTORATION

Gurmay Effrige Fraser

ARPress
45 Dan Road Suite 5
Canton MA 02021

Hotline:	1(888) 821-0229
Fax:	1(508) 545-7580

Ordering Information:

Quantity sales. Special discounts are available on quantity purchases by corporations, associations, and others. For details, contact the publisher at the address above.

Printed in the United States of America.

ISBN-13:	Paperback	979-8-89356-623-9
	eBook	979-8-89356-624-6

Library of Congress Control Number: 2024903447

Unless otherwise noted, all scripture quotations are from the Holy Bible, King James Version © 1982 by Thomas Nelson, Inc.

Table of Contents

Dedication — vii

Acknowledge — xi

Keep Breathing – God is not Finished with You Yet — 1

God Says It's The Beginning of Greatness — 16

Arrive To Survive To Thrive To Live — 28

Affliction of Abuse of my Vessel — 44

Facing the Giants in my Life That Fell and Died — 54

God's Plan is Still Inevitable Even in Broken Promises — 62

Endurance during the Years of Uncertainty — 76

Blessings Concealed in Abusive Relationships — 86

Reconnect To The Vine And Yearning to Belong — 95

The Dream Came Through At Its Appointed Time — 103

Transition into a New Beginning of the Unknown — 110

Single Parenting with Intimacy — 123

New Births of Rewards and Blessings in Parenting — 139

Searching For What's Missing — 145

Trials, Tributations, But Still Standing — 152

Overcoming Challenges of Life — 168

When Enough Is Enough? — 174

Not Who You Are But Who You Become — 185

Understanding God's Kingdom Principles — 195

Living The Greatest Years Ever – I'm Here Now — 205

Dedication

I dedicate my book, My Journey to Spiritual Restoration, to my Abba Father, to my beloved Jesus Christ of Nazareth, to the Holy Spirit, and to all the sons and daughters of God as we all pursue our spiritual restoration NOW.

God's blessings of Isaiah 61:1-11, upon my life, my children, our families, friends, and loved ones.

Isaiah 61:1-11 (KJV)

The Spirit of the Lord God is upon me; because the Lord hath anointed me to preach good tidings unto the meek; he hath sent me to bind up the brokenhearted, to proclaim liberty to the captives, and the opening of the prison to them that are bound;

To proclaim the acceptable year of the Lord, and the day of vengeance of our God; to comfort all that mourn;

To appoint unto them that mourn in Zion, to give unto them beauty for ashes, the oil of joy for mourning, the garment of praise for the spirit of heaviness; that they might be called trees of righteousness, the planting of the Lord, that he might be glorified.

And they shall build the old wastes, they shall raise the former desolations, and repair the waste cities, the desolations of many generations.

And strangers shall stand and feed your flocks, and the sons of the alien shall be your plowmen and vinedressers.

But ye shall be named the Priests of the Lord: men shall call you the Ministers of our God: ye shall eat the riches of the Gentiles, and in their glory shall boast yourselves.

For your shame ye shall have double; and for confusion they shall rejoice in their portion: therefore in their land they shall possess the double: everlasting joy shall be unto them.

For I the Lord love judgment, I hate robbery for burnt offering; and I will direct their work in truth, and I will make an everlasting covenant with them.

And their seed shall be known among the Gentiles, and their offspring among the people: all that see them shall acknowledge them, that they are the seed which the Lord hath blessed.

I will greatly rejoice in the Lord, my soul shall be joyful in my God; for he hath clothed me with the garments of salvation, he hath covered me with the robe of righteousness, as a bridegroom decketh himself with ornaments, and as a bride adorneth herself with her jewels.

For as the earth bringeth her bud, and as the garden causeth the things that are sown in it to spring forth; so the Lord God will cause righteousness and praise to spring forth before all the nations.

Acknowledge

Lord God, thank You so much for giving me the idea, inspiration, focus, joy, revelation, discernment, and strength to help me complete 'My Journey to Spiritual Restoration; and for using this Spiritual Memoire for "Changing Minds and Healing Nations."

I want to thank my children, Deon N Browne, MSIM, BS, and her husband, Kirkland G Browne, MBA, BS; and my son, Dawson D Joseph, Ph.D., MS, BS, for their love and encouragement, and sacrifices over the years and for supporting me in all my endeavors. My children, God bless all of you with excellent health and wholeness, a long, healthy whole life, the work of your hands, mind, and endeavors, and smile upon all of you always.

Thank you so much, my family, friends, and fans, for reading and reviewing my book, My Journey to Spiritual Restoration, and for sharing your excitement and your anticipation to see and feel it in your hands, and the hands of people global so they too can embark upon their journey to spiritual restoration. God bless us all continually.

Endorsement by

Pendergrass

Highly Recommended: It is an awesome book. By an incredible author. My Journey to Spiritual Restoration, is a very well writing book, it breaks my heart to read of what she went through, but her selflessness in sharing her experiences makes her life and her strength to overcome all she went through an inspiration for any who is lucky enough to read her story. I believe anyone who reads this book will realize they also have the strength to overcome any obstacle they face in their life as long as they are willing to give God their burdens. God tells us to lay our burdens at his feet and he will take care of them for us, just as this author has done. I cannot imagine how she has survived such a heartfelt life.

ESTHERCA

Spiritual Restoration for Us All. I really love your book. The entire time I was reading your book I imagined you as a baby and as a child growing up in Guyana and going through all the misfortunes you went through with your relatives. You are a brave person who suffered so much during your life, and I feel great that you overcame all of that. And you showed everybody that you can do anything with God`s love. Everyone should read your book.

jgarciadu

AMAZING COURAGE!!! A MUST READ!!!. The author of this book is remarkable! No matter what obstacles got in the way the determination to move forward in her life and let nothing bring her down is a true grace of GOD!! I was very touched and inspired by this book.

TBetts

Inspirational! The book is inspirational. It explains that no matter what happens God has the light to shine on all of us and heal the past. She is forthright on revealing atrocities in her life and how she worked through her faith to overcome and excel in life. She is a leader and spiritual beacon. The book will move and inspire those who read it to not give up, to be strong and work towards a happier future.

PKJBooks

Spiritual Restoration. My Journey to Spiritual Restoration, is a very well writing book, it breaks my heart to read of what she went through, but her selflessness in sharing her experiences makes her life and her strength to overcome all she went through an inspiration for any who is lucky enough to read her story. I believe anyone who reads this book will realize they also have the strength to overcome any obstacle they face in their life as long as they are willing to give God their burdens. God tells us to lay our burdens at his feet and he will take care of them for us, just as this author has done.

Anonymous

My Journey to Spiritual Restoration. My advice to anyone who is struggling is to first understand that life's challenges come to make you strong and if there is no challenge life begins to get boring. Therefore, step out of the frame of the picture of your life and look at the endless possibilities of your future and know that you can conquer and overcome any challenge that is presented to you. Even the storms of life have a season of where they have got to be calm and then just at those moments you take the authority of your life and divinely plan and walk into your destiny. You will then find your purpose and the things that God has created only you to change because you have that blueprint deep within the recess of your spirit. Don't allow anyone to steal your dream, your seeds, of greatness. As a single parent of two children, a certified special education teacher, a licensed psychotherapist, a certified motivational speaker and a best-selling author you can create an awesome life by bringing your future into your presence. Just begin to live your best life now regardless of your past. Your past is your past and there is nothing that you can do about it. However, you have control of your future.

Barbeejames; Linda Robinson Barbee, CEO Accounting, Bookkeeping & Tax Financial Services Plus, Inc.

My Journey to Spiritual Restoration. I've just completed reading the novel "My Journal to Spiritual Restoration", author Gurmay Fraser. The book reveals the marvelous work of God. Fraser, Arose As "A Women of True Courage and Faith". "My Journal to Spiritual Restoration" is a reminder to each of us that we must keep the faith, never give up, always be thankful for what God places in your life. Good or Bad each day is a new day and all that we can depend on is "God".

Each adversity faced by Fraser shows that God gave her the Strength to Endure". It was so inspirational to me. I read the entire book within a day; it was very difficult to put the book down. I could truly feel the presence of God in each word that was written in the book.

S_Hansen

A Must Read! Ms. Gurmay Fraser has endured more in her life than one person can ever imagine. This book allows you to push through whatever you are experiencing in your life that holds you in captivity. You want to be set free? you need hope, then read this book. Everyone of all ages!!!. The content of this book will allow you to breathe, live and have your being. Thank you, Ms. Gurmay, for being honest and transparent to allow others to break through what has been locked up inside for years. Wow and Wow.

Nniamey

My Journey to Spiritual Restoration Awesome. This book is truly inspiring! Ms. Fraser has gone through so much and she has been able to be victorious over every obstacle. If she can do it, so can I! As you read this book, you will realize that this book not only brings healing to your mind but to your spirit as well.

Charmaine11

My Journey to Spiritual Restoration Touching and Inspiring Book. Fraser has penned a great book about living out your destiny. She has proven to us that when God has a purpose for our lives there is nothing alive that can alter the course of our destiny to greatness. It is a book that everyone should read; especially, people who have experienced abuse, sickness and great emotional trauma. It gives hope to the hopeless. It makes you see the salvation of the Lord in the life of someone who people abused, misused and mistreated. While reading the book, I realized that if you are determined to overcome the obstacles and abuses you face in life, you can do so. God used the ordeal Fraser went through to make her the person she is today, and God navigated every rough terrain she had to go through. I was very touched by her story, and I pray that those who read it will focus on the message that is being presented. God is truly the author and the finisher of our faith, and this book proves it in so many ways. What a triumphant story!!!

ZDavis

My Journey to Spiritual Restoration Powerful Inspiration Book. I have been a therapist for over 21 years and feel this book will not only help people work through past abuse issues and inspire them to become the best they can be but also live their true dreams without any past emotional baggage. I will refer many friends and clients to purchase this AWESOME book.

Amazon Customer

In life we have the privilege to have people, situations, events, and media mold and impact our lives, but I am glad that I had the chance to have My Journey to Spiritual Restoration apart of that process. I am fortunate to have read and experience a book that has spoken to many dimensions in my spiritual walk, marriage and all other areas of my life. This masterpiece has unraveled many layers of hurt and shame to help set me free. Ms. Fraser's life helps uncover and reveal things that you may need to work on in your life to help you proceed to tackle your own journey. I thank Ms. Fraser for allowing God to use her life and story to help heal others. This is a must read for the whole family or anybody in the need of healing, restoration and rejuvenation. Thank you for your story because it has blessed my own.

P. Richardson

A powerful testament to faith. This book is a MUST read. Ms. Fraser's remarkable story is a true testimony of faith and how believing in God triumphs all things. By the end of the book, I felt renewed and inspired to continue the path of righteousness. Ms. Fraser teaches us the power of forgiveness, the importance of keeping the faith and CLAIMING God's favor. Each chapter offers another glimpse into her life and just when you think she is the victim, she becomes the VICTOR. If you are on a spiritual quest or are down and out and in need of spiritual upliftment, then this book is for YOU!

This book is a true testament of how faith in God and perseverance plays an important part in our lives when face with adversary and life obstacles. Ms. Gurmay's story has inspired me tremendously as well as my significant other who has experienced adversary and life obstacles. It goes to show that as human beings no matter how many times others try to destroy our lives, as long as we keep faith, do things the right way, and keep trying we will succeed. My Journey to Spiritual Restoration is definitely an excellent example of overcoming life obstacles no matter how bad we may think the obstacles are and should encourage us to continue Our Own Journey to Spiritual Restoration. What An Awesome Book.

Sandy

Great Book.

Kia

This is a powerful book that will inspire you to continue pressing on through your pain and struggles knowing that God has a specific plan for your life and your latter with be greater.

Godspoetic1

Will move you to tears, and heal you in your heart, mind and soul! "My Journey to Spiritual Restoration." Ms. Gurmay Fraser. When I first received the book, "My Journey to Spiritual Restoration", I was immediately touched by the title itself, as I think we all in one shape or form can relate to the need of a "spiritual restoration". Some people have even at one time or another in their lives, experienced a genuine "spiritual restoration". No matter how profound those life experiences have been that led up to that "spiritual restoration", what matters most, is that one made that journey to be restored and received it!

I was deeply touched by the author's life experiences that led her through her "spiritual restoration". I don't believe that many people could go through what she did, and come forth in the end, with such an awesome testimony of "spiritual restoration"! This book will move you to tears, and heal you in your heart, mind and soul! She is a true warrior and inspiration to women and children, all over the world facing the same issues every day, every hour, every minute! It is only with God's Grace & Mercy that will bring them all through!

As per FTC guidelines, I must state that I was given a copy of the book, "My Journey to Spiritual Restoration" from the author, in exchange for a review. My opinions are expressly my own and are in no way ever made positively or negatively, due to receiving a copy.

Mikka

I read this book twice and have been referring to it depending on what I was going through at the time. "My Journey to Spiritual Restoration" has given me a new perspective on life overall. There are clearly no limitations to what God can do no matter what the doctors or family may say and that became more evident when reading Gurmay's book. Initially my heart sank after learning of all the traumatic events Gurmay Fraser has experienced but as I continued to read, I began to get the big picture. A journey is a process usually related to a teaching, molding, and preparing for something. What I have been referring to in this book is how to get confirmation for what I think I'm supposed to be doing. (Thank You Gurmay Fraser!) I'm learning that God is continuing to put people in my life that are very influential of my own journey for spiritual restoration. God has also taken people out of my life that caused me to be unfocused. I truly appreciate this remarkable story as well as being able to know a true woman that is strong in faith and has succeeded in spiritual restoration.

Junie

Once again, we see the hand of GOD working in a miraculous way to preserve Gurmay so the world could hear her story, which undoubtly many of us can relate to. The book "My Journey to Spiritual Restoration" has capture the true essence of a woman's resilience journeying through a path of rough terrain on the way to her destiny...In spite of the shame, humility and abuse Gurmay is courageous as she candidly shares her life experiences, thus opening a doorway for abused victims/survivors to also take a step towards healing and restoration...Admittingly, I must applaud her for aspiring me to move forward where no one has gone before. May God continue to bless you in all your endeavors.

Shyluer Holder

For someone who have encountered so many near death experiences, abuse, molestation, rape, domestic violence, rejection from family members and others, and the list goes on; you are still standing in your right mind. WOW and WOW. This book is a must read for ALL. Men, Women and Children, if you have encountered anything in your life and don't know what to do, read this book and it will set the captives free. Freedom to Live, Breathe and Have your Being. She did it and so can You. Thank God for you Ms. Gurmay Fraser for being honest and transparent. God will continue to use you mightily to cause others to wake up to who they really are. GOD BLESS YOU to Infinite Infinity!!!

Lynden Hansen

My Journey to Spiritual Restoration is a must-read book. This book is a great example of how to persevere and keep hope despite your trials and tribulations. A book for all people regardless of age, race, sex, or religion. Everyone always told Ms. Fraser who she was (A nobody). By GOD's Grace and Spiritual Restoration Ms.

Fraser found out who she is (Intelligent, Awesome, Prosperous). Experience Your Journey to Spiritual Restoration!

Charisse

I initially started reading this book at a friend's house and I could not put it down. This book does not have a dull moment. I was truly amazed at her strength and courage to keep moving forward. Great ending and great book!

Davis

My Journey to Spiritual Restoration by Gurmay Fraser is a powerful spiritually inspiring book by a woman's personal true story of how she overcame many obstacles in her life including being poisoned, severe domestic violence and even surviving a near death experience only to live again not just physically but spiritually in order to inspire others.

Vivian A Clark

Inspired. This is a must read! Gurmay shared her personal journal of learning how to reach beyond the brokenness and betrayal as a child, in her marriage and much more. Gurmay's story inspired us as women to reach beyond the brokenness that we may have experience and to pull ourselves up until we reach a place of faith, peace and love.

John A. Abrams

I really love your book. The entire time I was reading your book I imagined you as a baby and as a child growing up in Guyana and going through all the misfortunes you went through with your relatives. You are a brave person who suffered so much during your life, and I feel great that you overcame all of that. And you showed everybody that you can do anything with God's love. With GOD we can overcome anything. Everyone should read your book.

Keep Breathing – God is not Finished with You Yet

My parents, John, my father, and Giver, my mother, met in Georgetown, Guyana, South America. The Giver was a single teenager in her mid-teens, beautiful brown complexion, medium built, about five feet five inches tall, and weighed about one hundred thirty pounds with a gorgeous afro hairstyle. In contrast, John was in his mid-twenties, about five feet nine inches, one hundred and sixty pounds, brown complexion, and beautiful soft black curly hair, with a slim statue. John is the second child in a family of seven. The Giver is the first child of seven other siblings. My mother met my father while attending secretarial classes after high school. During those days, my mother rode her bike to and from classes and enjoyed her life, friends, and social activities. John and Giver began to date, spent time together, and became involved in a relationship that evolved into physical intimacy. However, John was already married to someone else, and he and Giver continue their relationship of intimacy. John and Giver never married, nor did he divorce his wife.

Shortly after John and Giver's physical intimacy, Giver got pregnant and gave birth to their first child, a premature daughter weighing 3 pounds. This baby survived, and about fourteen months later, Gurmay was born.

I am Gurmay, the second child born to my parents. I was born a healthy full-term vaginal delivery 8 pounds 21 inches, light complexion with a full head of beautiful curly black hair, gray-green eyes, round face, in Berbice, New Amsterdam, Guyana, South America. I was told that I was a delighted and contented baby, I smiled a lot, and once I was fed and dry, I would entertain myself. I enjoyed my early morning outdoors when my mother, Giver, pushed me in my stroller before sunrise, and then I would nap for hours until it was time for me to be fed. During those times, Giver said I would love to listen to the musical toys attached to my crib. Many visitors came from near and far to set their eyes on me. I was a fair child and beautiful to behold. I would smile and equally engage with my visitors, giving steady eye contact. Giver said that I was so pleasant that sometimes she had to come and look to see what I was doing while lying in the crib because I would be so quiet enjoying the music of my toys. Many of the neighbors referred to me as the baby with a beautiful personality. All of that changed when I turned three months old.

Poisoned at Three Months Old

People often feel that things will always be how they are. But life and things should not be taken for granted. There are always seasons of change, and the changes that come are often unknown. But God is our assurance, for He said in his Word that if we put Him first and His righteousness, He would give us the desires of our hearts. Sometimes things we endure don't have to occur, but many times many parents are not on their watch, and they open their life and home to people without qualifying them. Many times, the warning signs and red flags are flying. Still, so many people and parents ignore them for several reasons, and children become victimized because parents ignore them and lack knowledge. While other times, parents and people want to minimize destructive behaviors and make excuses by justifying these bad behaviors. This was the beginning of the worse season of my life at the age 3-month-old.

Family that Hates Me

I was three-month-old when my 12-year-old female cousin, Boyer, pried my mouth opened and poured poison and acid down my throat. Boyer did not like me because of the color of my light skin and because I was a pleasant, happy, beautiful baby, and so many of the neighbors came by my mother's home to look upon me. My mother heard weird sounds coming from me shortly after my mother laid me down for my morning nap. My mother described the sounds as asphyxiation and choking sounds. Giver reported that during that time, she had a limitation with her gross motor skills and pain due to problems during my delivery. She would force herself to walk a short distance; even when she took me out in the morning, pushing me in the stroller, it was painful. So, when she heard choking sounds coming from me, she said that she didn't know where she got the inner strength from, and she forgot about the difficulty in walking. The next thing she knew, she was running up the stairs to my bedroom on the second floor, and to her horror, Boyer was smiling from ear to ear while holding the empty bottle of acid.

Be Strong and Very Courageous

Giver reported that she grabbed me up, wrapped me in a bedsheet, and tied me to her chest, and she quickly got on her bicycle and pedaled me to the hospital. I was sick and hospitalized for many months and lived in intensive care in the hospital in Berbice, New Amsterdam. Giver said that I lay lifeless during her visits to the hospital to see me, with minimal signs of movement or improvement. Because I was so young and tiny, there was not much the medical staff was able to do. I was unable to eat and had to be force-fed; unable to retain foods and liquids because I frequently expelled them from my tiny body. The medical staff could not try many medications or pump my stomach since I was a newborn in my first three months of life. After my hospitalization for so many months with little to no improvement, the medical team conference with my mother to discharge me. Finally, I was released with a poor prognosis to my teenage mother. I grew up with many health challenges, including problems with eating, digestion; enuresis, and severe learning problems that were evidenced by the slow rate of cognitive ability.

John and Giver Co-Parents

My mother moved several times from one location to another in the countryside and city of Guyana, South America. My parents never lived together. My dad would be described as a night visitor with many careers, but he spent many years working at the fire engine. My mother was a homemaker and did not work outside the house during that time. John and Giver continue their secret relationship, and my mother gave birth to three more children for John, for a total of five children that were born very close in age. My parents' relationship went from bad to worse when my fifth sibling was born.

3

John rarely financially supported my mother or their children. My mother had to go to his job on payday before the end of his workday to wait for him to give her financial support, or else she would not receive any money for children's aid. John then device a scheme, and he would escape through a different door to prevent my mother from seeing him so as not to give any financial support. My parents' relationship ended shortly afterward, and this caused severe economic pressure on my mother and her five children. With no means of financial survival, Giver had to create another plan to care for herself and her five children.

Season of Transition

Giver devised a plan to relocate to Maria, her mother's home, since getting a decent-paying job with little to no skill or formal education was impossible. As a single parent with five children in her early twenties, she had to find a way to quickly implement how she would prevent herself and her five children from escaping homelessness. Giver's plan, therefore, was to seek assistance from Maria by relocating to a different part of Guyana, South America, in the Northwest Region in Matthews Ridge.

My oldest sister and fifth sibling, John, jr. myself, and our mother, relocated to the countryside in Matthews Ridge in the Northwest Region to live with my maternal grandmother and her family. My younger brother and sister, third and fourth siblings, were left in the care of their godparents in Agricola, Georgetown, in Guyana.

In Matthews Ridge, we lived with our maternal grandmother, Maria, and her family in their crowded two-bedroom concrete flat. A partition separated this bedroom, and Maria, our grandmother, and her family shared the living room, kitchen, and bathroom with another tenant and their family. Our family was impoverished, but we never went hungry. There was always food to eat. Maria loved to cook and bake bread and cakes.

Family of Entrepreneurs

Shortly after my mother and three of her children relocated to Maria's home, my mother created a business cooking and selling bread, Ice blocks, and Flutie in the community. She went from house to house selling her baked goods and other edibles to create an income to support herself and the three children she brought from the city.

My grandmother had a business where she cooked breakfast, lunch, and dinner for about twenty-one single men. These men came to my grandmother's home Monday through Friday in the early morning to eat breakfast and collect their lunches placed in a flask for work. After work, they returned to my grandmother's home to return their flask and to eat dinner, and then they would go.

Giver and some of her siblings were culinary artists and bakers, dressmakers, or business owners, who raised pigs and chickens and sold pork, chickens, eggs, and other poultry. Giver's grandmother, Leila, owned an island, boat, and sawmill and employed many people to work her fields and sawmill. She supplied wood, fish, Copra, and many products to the neighboring islands and parts of Guyana, South America.

Giver Moved on

Many months later, my mother and one of these men got close enough and began to date to only dating each other. After some time, the dating continued into a relationship, and they both decided that Giver would move into his one-bedroom house with her infant, John, jr. Giver moved into this man's house with my infant brother and left my oldest sister and me to live with our grandmother, Maria, and our grandmother's family.

During this time, Giver became preoccupied with her life and the demands of a new relationship. The Giver was eight years younger than her new man, and her responsibilities now were altered from continuing her business to housekeeping and tending to this man's needs and the care of his house and her infant son. I rarely saw my mother during these times because she did not visit often, and we were not living close to each other for me to visit, and I was around 5-year-old, and I wouldn't know how to find my way to her house. Trains, taxis, and buses were not available in Matthews Ridge, and besides, I would have needed someone to take me to visit my mother. No one was available, and besides, I didn't want to ask my grandmother, Maria.

Fatherless and Motherless

John is gone, and now Giver is gone. I began to feel abandoned, intense fear, panic, grief, betrayed, detached, unloved, sad, angry, hopeless, helpless, insecure, unsafe, and unable to trust my parents and people. During this time, I displayed lots of doubt and frustration, and I often wondered why people get children when they are in no position to take care of themselves or their children. Why do people start a family when they are not committed? Many people start and continue a relationship because they say that they are in love. I question what happens when they are no longer in love. You don't start a relationship or marry someone because you love them only; so many people have no commitment to themselves or anyone. So that is why when they get involved in a relationship solely because of love when they fall out of love it is easy for them to leave the person and the relationship. In addition, they are not a commitment, and it is easy for them to leave because they are not invested in that relationship.

Children don't ask to be born, so I often wonder why mothers and fathers feel that they do their children a favor by conceiving and having children. Then these parents go their way and leave their children to clean up their mess; selfish mothers and selfish fathers.

Wolf in Sheep's Clothing

During the same time, one of the men that my grandmother, Maria, provided meals for, Mr. Young, also lived in her household and slept on the concrete floor of the living room. He was in his late forties, tall, brown complexion over 150 pounds, and homeless, a religious man he was called.

In the living room was an extra-large window, the only one that extended from one wall to the other and was made of a lattice. The insects, early morning chill, wind, rain, and the draft came through the lattice design that was the material of the window and made this room quite cold.

I was four years old and months, about 34 pounds and around 36 inches tall, slim body structure, and I suffered from enuresis and frequently wet my bed. Therefore, I was not allowed to share a space on the bed or floor in the bedroom next to my other family members.

I slept on the bedroom floor on a thin sheet separate from my other family members.

Nowhere to Lay my Head

My sleeping arrangement was changed. While my mother lived in the same house, I slept on the floor in the bedroom, separate from other family members but in the same space with other family members. Almost immediately after my mother left Maria, my grandmother's home, I was ordered to sleep in the living room on the concrete floor on a sheet in the dark, and it was so cold in the early morning. Also, the living room on the concrete floor is where Mr. Young slept.

Almost immediately, Mr. Young joined his bed next to my bed sheet and began inappropriately touching my private parts, kissing me on the lips, and physically restraining me from moving away from him or screaming. I immediately dragged my bed sheet away from his. He moved his bed closer to mine and joined it to my bed, then positioned himself on top of me while restricting my movements by using his hand to cover my mouth to prevent me from continuing to scream.

Planted in Bad Soil But it did not mean I was Not Good

The Rapist, Mr. Young, came to steal, kill, and destroy, and he threatened me not to say anything to Maria, my grandmother, Giver, my mother, or anyone else because he would hurt my family and me. I ignored his threats, fought him while I bit his hand, and wiggled my body from under him but was unsuccessful because his weight and body covered my tiny 4-year-old physical body. I was so scared and always afraid, panicky, angry, and sad. I was anxious when the night was approaching because I did not know what awaited me with rapist and child molester Young and I was afraid to sleep because of the unknown of what this rapist man would do.

At nights my anxiety levels were highest, and panic about the unknown with this child molester and the fear of closing my eyes to sleep made me exhausted, but eventually, sleep took over. Then I would become startled when I felt my body moving, and this would wake me, and I would be wide awake as rapist Young dragged the under ware off my body. I fought desperately to free my body from under the weight of his body on top of mine, but I was unsuccessful because Young, the

7

rapist's weight, was heavy on top of my tiny body that I felt suffocated. My pinches, scratches, and bites made no impact on this rapist's body.

Raped at 4 years old

Finally, Young succeeded in raping me, which became the beginning of the worse night of my life. This rapist succeeded in penetrating me with his private part. The pain was excruciating. I felt like my inside was coming out, and the pain felt like fire in my tiny body. Imagine living in the house with family, and they are all safely asleep, and I am being raped by this monster called Young that calls himself a man of his god. His weight suffocated me and pressed on my tiny body as I lay there helpless, wondering if I would survive to live. I was wondering if his weight had broken my rib cage. Rapist Young continued to rape me several nights during the week. During the daytime, when I saw him, I attempted to run far from his presence and find a safe place to hide and cry.

I became withdrawn from family and isolated myself. I had problems walking, going to the bathroom, eating, sleeping, focusing, and worry was frequent because I would be thinking of the bedtime ordeal with this rapist that my grandmother, Maria, allowed to be part of our family and have him sleep on the floor the exact location that she had me sleep.

Looking back, I often wonder why Maria, my grandmother, never came to check on my safety at night and why she was comfortable and trusting having this homeless man sleeping in the exact location. Or even why she would force me to sleep on this cold concrete floor in an area unsecure and away from family members? I was trapped, and many times when it was bedtime, I purposely fell asleep on the bed with my sister and family members in the bedroom, but my grandmother would wake me up and order me out of the bedroom to sleep on the living room floor where the rapist also slept.

Be Strong and Be of Good Courage

The devil, you are a liar, you tried to kill me at three months of age and now again at four years old, but devil, you will never succeed. Devil, you cannot defeat me because the real me is a spirit living in a body and the Holy Spirit lives in my body. God has created me in His

8

image and likeness, and everything that God has created and my Abba Father can never be defeated.

When I was scared, I reminded myself that my Abba Father was always with me. Hence, I became brave and bold one day and told my grandmother that Young was touching my private parts, taking off my clothes, laying on top of me, and putting his private part in my private part. My grandmother hit me in my mouth and told me never to tell lies about this godly man and never to say anything to anyone about this matter.

My grandmother ordered me to continue to sleep on the living room floor away from our family that slept in the bedroom, and rapist Young continued to rape me for several months.

Reunited with Giver

Many months later, my mother, Giver, came to get my older sister and me, and she moved us into the house with her and her partner, Ralph. We went to live with our mother, Ralph, her partner, and our infant brother. My mother later gave birth to two sons for Ralph, and now my mother has seven children: three daughters and four sons. My brother and sister left living with their godparents in Agricola Village and joined us in Matthews Ridge Northwest Region in the country in our one-bedroom house, and now we were living in a crowded space.

What is my Purpose?

Many times, I asked myself, what is my purpose? Indeed, my Abba Father did not create me in His image and His likeness and formed me from a rib of man and sent me to earth to be poisoned, raped, and abused; this should be my purpose. Oh no! I had to rethink how to reposition myself in a fertile environment because I am a good seed, and it doesn't matter how good the seed is; if you remain in an environment that is not conducive to your destiny, then you will become a product of that environment that it will limit you from destine.

I'm reflecting on how my life has transformed from the beginning and the experiences that have shaped and changed me into who I am. I am the second of seven children. The Bible states that the number two "conveys the meaning of a union, division or the verification of facts by

9

witnesses. A man and woman, though two in number, are made one in marriage (Genesis 2:23 - 24)."

My life had a very humble beginning. As I reflect on the afflictions of my life, I'm amassing them to see how they point me in the direction of God's perfect plan, the purpose of my life. To God is the glory! It is amazing that I am alive, still standing, and in my right mind. I was born with normal full-term gestational delivery.

Have you or anyone you know ever-experienced child abuse?

Physical abuse

Do you know of anyone that was poisoned? _____

_____

_____

_____

_____

What would you have done if your child was poisoned at 3 months old? _____

_____

_____

_____

_____

Did you or your child/ren's life was ever interrupted due to physical abuse? _____

_____

_____

_____

_____

Emotional abuse

Have you experienced prejudice in the job, community, church, school, family or home? _____

_____

_____

_____

_____

Imagine you giving birth to a healthy child and someone resenting this child because of the color of his/her skin; what would you do? _____

_____

_____

_____

_____

How would you feel if someone didn't like you because of your skin color? _____

_____

_____

_____

_____

Have any of your children complain of their peers not liking them because of their ethnicity, beliefs, tradition, living arrangements? ___

_____

_____

_____

_____

What happens if your family or in-laws didn't like your child's color?

_____

_____

_____

_____

_____

What would you do if your family shows favor to one of your children more than another? _____

_____

_____

_____

_____

Have you ever been rejected by your family, friends, church? _____

_____

_____

_____

_____

How would you handle rejection? _____

_____

_____

_____

_____

Attempted Murder

Imagine you put your 3-month-old baby for their morning nap and suddenly you hear your baby making panicking choking sounds, what would you do? _____

_____

_____

_____

_____

What would you imagine happen to your baby? _____

_____

_____

_____

_____

To make matters worse, you have problems walking and climbing stairs what would you do? _____

_____

_____

_____

_____

Now when you finally got up the stairs you see your baby gasping with froth coming from their mouth and nose and their face covered in it. What would be your first reaction? _____

_____

_____

_____

_____

How would you react if your infant was poison? _____

_____

_____

_____

_____

Imagine your cousin or family member or babysitter prying your baby's mouth open and pouring poison down their throat what would your response be? _____

_____

_____

_____

Can you imagine seeing your baby's neck burnt with a scar? _____

_____

_____

_____

Now your baby's body inside and outside is physically damaged, would you be afraid to touch your baby? _____

_____

_____

_____

Now your family's life is interrupted because your baby is hospitalized and lives in the intensive care unit with barely any sign of recovery. What are your thoughts, feelings and emotions? _____

_____

_____

_____

How would you be able to help your baby that is unable to eat and needs to be forced fed? _____

_____

_____

_____

How would you feel because your baby is unable to retain food and fluid? What are your thoughts? _____

_____

_____

_____

_____

Months later your baby is discharged from the hospital with poor prognosis, and very little improvements, what would you do? _____

_____

_____

_____

How would you take care of your baby that even the medical professionals cannot care for? _____

_____

_____

_____

Advice for Parents

Did you have any crisis as a child? _____

_____

_____

_____

Have you experienced any near-death experience or know of anyone that did? _____

_____

_____

_____

Did your son or daughter experience any crisis when they were born or while they were infants, toddlers, etc.? _____

_____

_____

_____

Did your child/ren or your life ever been interrupted due to abuse, rejection, abandonment, trauma or neglect, etc.? _____

_____
_____
_____
_____

What advice would you give to your family or friends to ensure that their children are safe even from family members? _____
_____
_____
_____
_____

If your child or grandchild suffered from abuse, how would you handle this? _____
_____
_____
_____
_____

How do you parent or co-parent your child/ren? _____
_____
_____
_____
_____

What advice do you have for parents, family and friends, or even co-workers or educators on educating children about safety? _____
_____
_____
_____
_____

Do you have any advice for parents allowing other people living in their home? _____
_____
_____
_____
_____

God Says It's The Beginning of Greatness

My recovery from the rape, molestation, and pain in my body was very slow. I never shared the rape, pain, or molestation with my mother or anyone else for fear that I would be doubted, not believed, or smacked for saying that I was lying on this god-fearing man; also, I fear I would be doubted and ostracized.

Abode with Giver and Her Partner

Living with my mother, Ralph, her partner, and my siblings was okay; for one, I felt emotionally and physically safe. The one-bedroom house was tiny. The living room and bedroom were in one location. But the kitchen was in the yard, separated from the bedroom and living room in a building all by itself. We had no running water, electricity, bathroom, toilet, fan, or air conditioner. The bathroom was a small building in the yard all by itself; the toilet was called a latrine, a small building over a pit, and the seat was cut in a large oval shape that you sat over. I had nightmares for years after, as I remember having to peep into that black hole into a bottomless pit before sitting over it. I was always fearful that I would fall into this pit, and no one would know where I was so they could come to rescue me.

Developmental Milestone

My development was slow and delayed, and I had many problems with eating and sleeping. My mother was told I would never be normal, let alone live a normal life. I had difficulties in other developmental areas in my life except for motor skills; I walked independently. I reacted negatively to sensory input; even today, I still have some degree of negative reaction to sensory input. I struggled in kindergarten. My cognitive ability was delayed; I had problems recognizing numbers and letters, writing the alphabet was a struggle, and I reversed many letters and numbers when I wrote them. I had trouble recalling letters, numbers, colors, shapes, and lots of issues with tactile stimulation.

I grew up as a loner; it seemed that I never really fitted in even though I tried. Even though I was from a large family, I never felt I belonged. I never knew what it was. It always seemed as though everyone was too busy with their affairs, and when I came around them, I felt I was bothering them. Therefore, I would end up spending much time by myself. Looking back, I realized I had feelings of abandonment for many years, not realizing that I was not sent to fit in but to stand out. I was trying to fit into situations, mindsets, and environments that were too limited and small for the anointing that God has placed in and on my life.

First time John Abandoned Me

My family gatherings included picnics and a family picnic on the East Bank of Demerara in a field close to the airport when I was around two years old, something happened. I remembered standing there in a diaper as I watched my family mingle with each other. On this occasion, I remembered my father, John telling me that he was going to the store and would bring me back candy (sweetie). After he left for the store, he never got the candy and never returned that day. I waited and expected to see my dad return, but he didn't, and I did not see him again until many years later.

For many years I have wondered why my dad never returned with the candy he had promised. Did I do something wrong? Was I not good enough as his little girl? Was I not pretty enough? Did he not love me? Who will protect me and keep me safe from the wickedness of people? Why did he abandon me? Was I not fair enough? Was something wrong with my appearance, my color, and my looks? Why has he not returned to see about me? To celebrate my achievements in life. I thought that because we shared the same birthday month and date, we would always honor our birthday together. For many years I waited for my dad to return, and he never did for many years, not even a letter or postcard or an appearance at my school or during the holidays like Christmas, Easter, or any family events. My dad just went missing, and no one, not even my mother, Giver, is saying anything about him.

I know he visits because my mother has three other children after me, and I heard the gossip that they are his, but when he is visiting or coming to the house, I have never seen him in the daytime.

I'm his only child that looks just like him. I always felt different, and this feeling was always there. I still remember how sad I felt with the absence of John in my life, and I could not tell anyone about my thoughts and feelings.

Suffering in Silence

My father's departure from my life caused me lots of anxiety, fear, issues with trust, abandonment, detachment, feelings of panic, feelings of desperation, and insecurities. This led me to feel that parents and caregivers couldn't be trusted, and then I realized that I couldn't trust others to take care of me, and I had to take care of my life and felt the need to protect myself at all costs if I wanted to feel and to be safe. I also realized that quitting myself was not an option.

As I got older, I continued to suffer medically, experienced digestion and bloating problems, and had many social and academic problems. I always felt responsible for caring for myself and couldn't leave that responsibility to anyone.

In my culture, children were taught to be responsible at very early ages; chores were assigned that had to be completed daily, or else my mother or caregivers would use the rod of correction, a whip or cane, to beat me for not following the instructions and for disobedience.

I could not be fully toilet trained before age two; I suffered from enuresis, the repeated voiding of urine day and night in my clothes and bed. This continued into my teenage years. I had challenges with digestion and suffered from bloating problems.

I had difficulties with communication skills, including comprehending and retaining information. I had difficulties putting words together, processing them verbally, and responding to questions and comments. When I attempted to speak, I was told to "shut up."

I suffered from low self-esteem, low self-confidence, poor social skills, insecurities, and very shyness. Doctors were unable to correct my enuresis and learning problems.

Poverty is a Curse

I came from a poor family with limited resources. My mother was a housewife; my father did several jobs, including driving a taxi and working at the Fire Department – when he did work. My mother struggled to get child support money for the five children they had together.

My father was an alcoholic and an adulterer, and when he visited in my absence, either while I was in school or asleep, he left again until years later. When my father, John, abandoned the family and both of my parents split up, my fifth sibling was three months old. This caused severe hardship to my family since he refused to provide emotional and financial support for us.

My father disappeared, and my mother was now responsible for raising the children alone without any support and resources. Guyana, my native country, had no entitlement programs: no food stamps, public assistance, Supplemental Security Income, low-income housing, Section 8 housing, food pantry, or support for the single parent, period. If you didn't work, you didn't eat. No childcare services were available or jobs for unskilled citizens; therefore, my mother had to decide for herself and her children and create entrepreneurial opportunities for us to arrive to survive, thrive, and live.

Called but not Chosen

I now understand that God elects some parents to carry the seed and some to fertilize the seed, while other parents are assigned to do both – that is their assignment, period. When I look at the life that John, my biological father, lived, I am blessed that God did not choose him to raise me because he was not qualified to raise a Kingdom seed name Gurmay. I am so thankful that God is Father to the fatherless, and God is my Daddy. I have never called any man daddy, and I always wondered that daddy was reserved for God only, my Abba Father.

I am so thankful to God that God used my biological father to fertilize the seed because it now has dawned on me that God could not have chosen a greater man, John. My father was very ambitious and skilled; sadly, he never knew God's purpose for his life. I say this sincerely.

During the sporadic time that I spent with John, my father, I could see and feel the love he had for me; even in the way that he spoke to me and, how he looked at me when he spoke with me, how he embraced me when he held me and when he touched me. I thank God for my biological father's obedience because I would not have been born if he had not participated in God's plan to fertilize the Kingdom seed.

When my father left, he was gone much longer, and his whereabouts were unknown. My family struggled because we were just so poor at that time, but we never went hungry or without the basic resources to sustain our life.

Looking back, I feel I did not give my mother enough credit for keeping my four siblings and me together. My mother was many years younger than my father and was in school when my father met her. She fell in love with him, and the rest is history.

Questions for you to Reflect

What would you do if you were told that your baby would not survive?

_____

_____

_____

_____

_____

How would you react if you were told that your baby would not do normal things like her/his peers? _____

_____

_____

_____

_____

Or if your baby survives, the baby will not live a normal life? _____

_____

_____

_____

_____

Did you have challenges with sleeping or eating as a child? _____

_____

_____

_____

_____

Did you experience any cognitive delays as a child? _____

_____

_____

_____

_____

How would you feel if you were unable to perform reading, writing, and mathematics? _____

_____

_____

_____

_____

How do you feel if your child was unable to engage with his/her environment? _____

_____

_____

_____

_____

How should that baby interact with their family, school and community?

_____

_____

_____

_____

_____

What are the possible problems you believe such a baby would have?

_____

_____

_____

_____

_____

As the parent of that baby, what are possible ways that you could help your child to integrate into the school and community? _____

_____

_____

_____

_____

How would you feel if you heard your child is dumb, stupid, retarded
or not able to learn? _____

_____

_____

_____

_____

Do you have cousins? _____

_____

_____

_____

Are you an introvert or extrovert? _____

_____

_____

_____

Imagine you are this little girl and your family and friends not wanting
to be seen next to you, what would you do? _____

_____

_____

_____

What is your relationship with your father? _____

_____

_____

_____

What is your relationship with your mother? _____

_____

_____

_____

Have you been rejected by any of your parents? _____

_____

_____

_____

_____

How and when? _____

_____

_____

_____

_____

Have your parents ever promised you anything and not fulfill that promise? _____

_____

_____

_____

_____

How did that make you feel? _____

_____

_____

_____

_____

Did you feel unheard by their action? _____

_____

_____

_____

_____

What is your relationship with your siblings? _____

_____

_____

_____

_____

What is your relationship with your cousins? _____

_____

_____

_____

_____

If your cousin poisoned you, would you have a relationship with your cousin? _____

_____

_____

_____

Would you be able to forgive your cousin? _____

_____

_____

_____

Would you interact with your cousin's mother and her family? _____

_____

_____

_____

Would you want to eat from her? _____

_____

_____

_____

Would you be able to love her? _____

_____

_____

_____

Would you confront her? _____

_____

_____

_____

What were the worse feelings of rejection or abandonment you've felt as a child? _____

_____
_____
_____
_____

Who rejected or abandon you? _____
_____
_____
_____
_____

What is your relationship with this person now? _____
_____
_____
_____
_____

Have you experienced any health challenges as a child? _____
_____
_____
_____
_____

How did you deal with those challenges? _____
_____
_____
_____
_____

Did you ever feel that you were responsible to care for yourself as a child? _____
_____
_____
_____
_____

How many siblings do you have? _____
_____
_____
_____
_____

What number are you? _____

_____

_____

_____

_____

As a child did you feel emotional or physically safe? Why? Why not?

_____

_____

_____

_____

_____

Were your parents emotionally available to you? _____

_____

_____

_____

_____

Were your parents emotionally present with you? _____

_____

_____

_____

_____

Did you have chores as a child? _____

_____

_____

_____

_____

How old were you when you were assigned to chores? _____

_____

_____

_____

_____

Was there organization in your home? _____

_____

_____

_____

_____

Did your parent/s hold you accountable for your behavior? _____

_____

_____

_____

_____

Arrive To Survive To Thrive To Live

As I reflect on our journey to the countryside of Matthews Ridge in the Northwest Region, it was an agonizing trip. This was due to the lack of resources and finances; my mother, my siblings, and I arrived by boat and train. This trip started in Georgetown, Guyana, on Monday afternoon on the Lady North Court, the name of the ship that sailed to Morawhanna, then we got on a smaller boat to Port Kaituma. Afterward, we took a train to Matthews Ridge on Thursday afternoon. Then we got a ride to Maria, my grandmother's house.

I remembered feeling so lost and displaced. We were strangers in the country to live with a family we did not know how they would embrace us. Even though I was only four years old, I felt that our family saw Maria and her children as strangers too. Looking back at my arrival in Matthews Ridge, in the country and the experiences I've gained there made me realize that God created me for greatness. I know that just surviving is not an option for me, ever!

Just Surviving is not Enough

For ever so long, and as far as I can remember, I made up my mind a long time ago that I was not created to survive. Too many people are just surviving and accepting whatsoever life throws at them. I believe that the mere fact that I was born when I did, I have already beat the odds to survive. Can you imagine the millions of sperm cells that have competed to fertilize the egg that has developed into me? My egg was called, chosen, appointed, set apart, anointed, blessed, and my egg beat all the odds of the other eggs and was fertilized by that sperm that beat all the millions to meet my egg, and only that specific sperm succeeded over the millions that it competed against.

Don't Give up on You

God has not and never will give up on me. Therefore, I would never give up on myself either. I believe that I was resilient before I was even born because my mother had to overcome so many adversary situations, especially with John, my biological father, and his family. I have made up my mind from the age of 2 years old that regardless of what happens to me in my life's journey, I will make it and be just fine because I know that I am the apple of my God's eyes and God will always protect me because He said He would never leave me nor forsake me.

I had suffered from persecutions starting from three months old when I was deliberately poisoned, was sick for many years, and suffered many different medical diagnoses. Then again, at four years old when I was brutally raped for many months, bullied in school from elementary right through to high school, ostracized by my very family for having my independent thoughts, and raped at the age of 16 years old because I refused to agree to marry Bert.

To navigate my life's journey, I must be resilient even in the face of persecution, and I must know that life itself is not a harbor but a journey. For me to get anywhere in my life, I must keep it moving and speaking to my mountains because I know that when I come in the name of Jesus Christ of Nazareth, no one or nothing can stand before me, period, and I believe this.

Resilience

When I recalled the persecutions that I've faced in my life, initially, it made me very angry, but once I began to have a relationship with God, my Daddy, I realized that these are all part of God's perfect plan for me. Resilience builds my faith because the faith that is not tested cannot be trusted, and knowing this has helped me bounce back very quickly from what appears to be negative experiences and has allowed me to thrive and rise to the top. I have become very self-aware to understand my weaknesses and manage those, my values, strength, clarity, the importance of self-care, emotional and physical health, and wellness. Also, I begin to spend time with myself, use my imagination to create things and situations, and realize that God has given me the power and authority to change any position that does not align with God's purpose for my life.

My attention began to focus more on me and not the negative things that people speak about me because I know that God's anointing in and on my life frightens people but that they must deal with it. After all, there is nothing they can do about it.

Persecutions Come and Must Leave

All persecutions have a time and season, and expiration date. As I recall the persecutions, they remind me of being in a picture, and while in that picture, you cannot see the frame. Therefore, making decisions is difficult. They may not serve me well because they would be based on my emotions.

Wickedness in School Leadership

I was frequently bullied in high school because of my Guyanese accent, British accent, and even spelling and pronunciation of many words and how I wrote the date then. I was frequently teased and told to go by on the banana boat to wherever I came from because Brooklyn, New York, didn't want people like me. Many of the students were cruel, and they did not hesitate to speak ill or use their bodies to rush up to me and past me, making sure they hit me. In the beginning, I was always in a fight or flight mode. At that time, my brother and sister attended the same high school but saw us together, and you would not know that we lived in the same household or that we were John and Giver's, children. They ignored me completely, and I always tried to engage them until they made it clear that I should have stayed back in Guyana because now they must share their resources and stuff with me, and they were quite unhappy. I believe if I had indulged in cutting classes, smoking marijuana, going to the dollar rammer parties, and drinking, I would have been accepted. I chose not to.

Education System that Underserved Me

When I believed things would get better as I stayed focused on high school graduation and attending continuing education classes to stay out of the way of my brother and sister, I received news that shook me up. I struggled academically in high school. My high school guidance counselor summons me, and this was April month to meet with her. At that meeting, she told me that she had made a mistake, incorrectly calculated my credits, and realized that I was short of a physical education class. This delayed my graduation, which should have been in June, in two months to January the following year.

I burst into tears and became so angry with her and the education system. How do they have incompetent working on these jobs and no one is supervising them or holding them accountable. At that moment, I then had to encourage myself and make an oath that I would return to be a teacher to save students from incompetent staff like her and her supervisor. I eventually graduated and was quite happy to get out of that school to embrace college life. Still, I was very hesitant with some anxiety to know if I would ever embrace a similar experience.

Abuse of Authority in Colleges

Within a few months, I then enrolled in my first community college. There I struggled with the entrance examinations in Mathematics and Reading, and finally, after retaking these tests and taking remedial classes, I passed those tests. The courses were challenging, and I struggled from the beginning to keep up with the homework and examinations. I was seen as an average "D" student, and I continued to struggle. But I continued to work hard, but it was not good enough. I attended extra classes and tutoring and even inquired about any service for students that are struggling, but nothing was offered to me.

Courage to Stand in the Storm

Finally, I was writ to the dean's office and was handed a letter and was told that I was academically expelled due to poor academic performance of my grade point average of under 2.000. I was never offered any options before this engagement with the dean. I was told that I could reapply in six months and hope my application would be accepted to return to the community college and the guidelines would be given to me then. I did apply and was accepted, and I worked my butt off, and I finally graduated with a 2.300-grade point average.

Courage to go After my Dream

I then applied to attend a four-year university, and I was so afraid that I would not be accepted because I was often told that I was not college material. However, it is not what people say about me that matters. What I say about myself and what I believe about myself makes the difference. I was accepted to a four-year university on provisional status, and the requirements were established for the first semester: two A's and one B, my first semester. Anything different, I would be let go at the end of that semester. At the end of that semester, I got two A's and one B's, and I was approved to continue my Advance Standing Bachelor of Science Degree. And I did graduate in two years with a high-grade point average. It was not by might nor by power but by the Holy Spirit in me that kept me strengthened and focused on graduating, and I had to change my mindset about who God said I am.

Be Strong and be of Good Courage

I needed five professional references to be attached to my graduate application to grad school. Before graduation, I asked one of my professors for a reference for grad school. He remarked that I should be contented with my Bachelor of Science and stay focused on being a single mother to my two children. He refused to give me that reference, and he never did.

I acquired all five references, applied to grad school, and was accepted; one year later, I graduated Magna Cum Laude with my master's degree in social work. I have learned that people's opinion of me has nothing to do with my opinion. I am justified by my words.

Environments that denied me

I've endured the abuses while working in New York with a demonstration of abuse of leadership and authority figures. My first public school teaching experience was great until I stood up for unrighteous behaviors. Another student with a pencil stabbed a second-grade student, and that student sat in the class with blood oozing from his finger. I was a teacher at the same school, and I happened to go to the classroom to ask the teacher a question when I saw this little African American boy sitting on his seat crying. His complexion was pallor. Therefore, I directed my attention to him and insisted that the teacher do something about it, and I did not leave the classroom until the teacher did. This Caucasian teacher reported that I interrupted his class and did not mind my business. My supervisor brought me into a conference with the principal and the assistant principal and disciplined me and demanded that I should sign this form that they would place in my files. I refused to sign any form; from that moment, they made my life hell.

About two months later, one of my students purposely pushed his chair into my right kneecap and almost shattered my knee. I was sitting in the back of the student, assisting him with his class work. Two of my staff wrote an accident report and signed and dated what they saw because they and I had copies for their records, and I kept the originals. The school nurse administered first aid, and I took her original statement for my records. The school administrator refused for me to leave to seek medical assistance, and I was detained to work until the end of the day before I was able to go to the emergency room. X-rays were done; by that time, my knee and leg were swollen to the size of a small pumpkin. I returned to work the day after, and that was my last day at work as a special educator after years of teaching. I received medical care, and I held them accountable with legal action.

Success Breaths Contempt

Another experience as a psychotherapist landed me a job with a nonprofit agency. Mismanagement of their funds should have been their first name. During my first six months working there, they would direct deposit my paycheck and reverse the direct deposit. It was now Christmas, and the director deposited my salary and reversed it. When I showed up to work and inquired about my salary, I was informed that they don't have sufficient funds to pay everyone, and since I am new to the company, I would have to wait until after Christmas to get paid. When they finally paid my salary in the new year, I gave notice and kept it moving.

Stop Remaining in Stuffs too Small to Embrace Your Vision

My next job was working for the federal government, which was quite an experience. I was supposed to be a people pleaser to accept abuse and be thankful that they hired me. My job assignment was changed many times, the boss pleasers stayed in the office, and I was frequently in the field more than many of my colleagues. It came to a collision path when I had surgery from the incident while teaching when my right knee was damaged. My director promised that she would accommodate me to work in the office after surgery and to have to wear a hard brace that extended from my thigh to my ankle that I had to wear for eight weeks. To my shock, when I returned to work a week after surgery, I did work in the office, and the second week I was sent into the field. I reminded her of the verbal contract, and she said that she had changed her mind, and there I was, taking trains and buses and hopping, and my first assignment was at a client's home on the ninth floor and the elevator was broken. I had to walk up nine flights, sweating and crying. I left this job and returned to the school system in the hope that things would be better.

Seed Grows When it is placed in Something Bigger Than Itself

My new job was at a high school providing social work services to students in special education was different. I covered four different school locations in this assignment, which was very stressful, but I did well and enjoyed my assignments. The climate changed instantly when the principal at this school approached me on the last school day. He was coming in my direction, and I was going in his direction to greet some of my colleagues when he walked into me and kissed me on my lips. I smelled strong alcohol when he opened his mouth to tell me that he fought to have me at his school and the hospital program for five days, and I, therefore, did not have to cover the other schools. He then asked me what I was going to give him in return. I pushed him out of my way, and he gave me the nastiest mean look as I rushed away from him to reach.

Stop Playing it Safe and Stand up Against Unrighteous Acts

This was the beginning of the worse days at this school location. A few weeks into the Fall school year, he ordered me into his office. He told me that one of the students on my caseload was a pain in the security guards and staff's "butt," He wanted me to do an assessment for this student and to include that he didn't belong here and required a more restrictive school environment. The principal requested that I should falsify this report and create stuff so that this student would be

34

placed elsewhere. I told him that this student's behaviors fit the school placement and that this student is no different from the other students.

Break The Unjust Rules

The principal said he expected me to follow his orders or else. I told the principal that I refused to falsify any report and would not do it. The following things I know are the principal called a meeting with my supervisor and superintendent of the district on a day when I was not assigned to his site. His secretary called me and said that the principal demanded that I attend a meeting now and with my chain of command. I told his secretary that I'm assigned to the off-site currently and asked why he had not set an appointment when I was at his site any of the three days. The principal was standing there and heard me and began to yell that he expected me to leave and come right away. I then responded that if something happened to any of those students in my absence, it would be my license since he did not give me an official letter with an agenda to prepare for the meeting. He began to scream that he would put something in my file because I was insubordinate. I told him that he was disrespectful and was abusing his authority and that he had planned a meeting and wanted me to attend but did not give me a written notice or an agenda even though I was at his side the day before. Therefore, I have declined to attend because I felt I was being set up and would be attending a meeting in the absence of my union representative.

Get Out of my Way

The principal did all kinds of unjustifiable behaviors to get me fired. He changed the time that I had to report to work and said I was not writing progress notes. I told him that he was the school's principal, but he was not my supervisor. Therefore, my notes should be handed to my supervisor, not to him. He then summoned my supervisor and the superintendent to pay me an unannounced visit. They came unannounced, and they knocked on my office door wanting to speak with me, and I denied them access because they were supposed to give me notice, and I needed to have my union representative present. They then asked me why I did not share the problem at the school with the principal and them. I told them the reason I did not share with them is the same reason they did not share with me that they were invited to a meeting about me, and they failed to inform me because they are friends with the principal and are unable to be objective. I told them I don't trust their judgment, and their behaviors have proven my suspicion.

The Battle Belongs to the Lord

I met with the principal face to face on one of my rounds to bring a student to my office for social work services, and in my mind, I said that the principal continues to harass me because I refuse to be his bed partner. Still, my God will choose who will remain at this site, either he or me. I was assigned to the other location on the last day of school. The secretary called and said that the principal called for a rapid emergency dismissal. When I arrived, he was in the auditorium on the stage, and we all sat quickly; and he announced that today was his last day there. He burst into tears because the superintendent fired him. According to God's Word in Psalm 105:14-15 (KJV), He suffered no man to do them wrong: yea, he reproved kings for their sakes; Saying, Touch not mine anointed, and do my prophets no harm.

Searching for Fulfillment in my Life

I was happy to move to the South to start a new life and to have a better and peaceful experience, to be respected and allowed to do my job, or so I thought. My focus was to expand my social work skills in a different location and with different clients. The encounter of the many persecutions received.

Abuse in North Carolina Workplaces

My First Psychotherapy job had so many uncertainties; I thought it would be the best since the Chief Executive Officer was an Elder at his church. However, it did not unfold that way. The first time I took an earned day off, he called me to inquire and left a message asking why I needed to take off. I refused to return an answer to his message. When I showed up to work the following day, he was annoyed and told me he expected me to return his call. I responded that I did not see that expectation in the employee handbook.

Next, he requested that I should share my state login credentials with his new staff, and I refused. He rushed into my office while I was staffing clients' cases with his team by interrupting the meeting and told me to pack my stuff, clean out my office and get out of his office. I told him that he was wicked and good at firing staff members on the phone. I told him that God would hold him accountable for his abusive behaviors. He lost both contracts shortly after, and his businesses were shut down.

After this experience, I've worked for eight other mental health agencies. They were terrible, besides abusing their leadership, not paying salary for a time earned, increasing duties, making an unreasonable requests violating their employee's contract, and showing no accountability.

My worse experience was working as a high school teacher. Initially, I had one prep. I was teaching one course my first and second semesters. At the beginning of the third semester, I was transferred to a new program where school leadership placed all emotionally challenged students, some of them in and out of detention, excessive in and out of school suspension and probation, and ankle braces into a program away from the main high school campus. These students were not allowed to mix with mainstream students.

All these Things Will Work For my Good

The conditions at this building were deplorable; no separate teachers' bathroom or lunchroom were available. Teachers had to open and close the building daily. One of the most frightening experiences was early in the morning, it was pitch dark outside the building, and all the bulbs had blown. The school leadership was informed, and no bulbs were replaced for months. Huge trees surrounded this building and from where you park your vehicle to the entrance door was quite a distance in the pitch dark. Other deplorable conditions were the ceiling had big holes and cracks, and when it rained, the teachers had to place garbage bins to collect water. The heat was broken in half of the building, and they were electric heaters to heat the room, and teachers and students had to keep their coats on. If not, the temperature would be too cold to remain in the building. Rats were running in the classrooms, which was not a concern to the administrators.

In my third semester, I had two preps and was mandated to teach two different courses. To my horror, in my third and fourth semesters, I was mandated to teach four courses: Marketing, Sports and Entertainment Marketing, Principles of Business and Finance and Entrepreneurship, and writing four different lesson plans daily and twenty a week along with creating twenty online classes a week. If you think this was bad, I was told that I was not working hard enough, and I was then mandated to monitor students in these four subjects: English, Maths, Science, and Social Studies.

The Will Come to me one Way but Flee in 7 Different Ways

Then to make matters worse, I was harassed by one of the high school leaders to falsify a peer review of me by one of the teachers. I refused, and all kinds of letters were placed in my online file. All sorts of threatening letters came to my home address, and emails were sent to me about signing this document. I did not budge, and I never signed it.

Things got worse because one day, while I was teaching students in the four different courses and monitoring the other students in the four different subjects, I was there alone with these students with the worst behavioral problems. The worse fear came through when one of the students continuously interrupted my class, and even though I asked her to stop, she began to use all kinds of profanity and threatening language at me. She refused to stop; therefore, I got on the computer to write her up. Unbeknownst to me, she snuck up behind me. I heard a weird sound, and when I turned to my left side, she was so close to my chair that I was prevented from moving. She stated that she will teach this mother F... a lesson that I will never forget. She announced that she would pull the electric cord of the computer from the wall so that my report would disappear. Now I'm sitting, but in a twisted position, she threatened me and used all kinds of profanity while the entire class of students watched on. No staff member or security was present. The next thing I know, she threw her body over the left side of my body, and her weight came on top of my back, and I sustained two dislocated discs in the left side of my neck, a torn shoulder cuff, and five dislocated discs in my spine. The school administrators have never inquired about my health or well-being. Instead, the school administrators referred me to the police because I did not show up to work the second day even though the school secretary received all the doctors' notes.

Abuse of Church Leaders

Volunteering at churches can be very intimating for pastors. My experience as a Servant of God came to a collision path when the pastor of a church where I preached and teach bible study released me from her church because she said my anointing was too powerful. The congregation looked up to me and did not listen to her. She called me to report that she released me because I disrespected an elder by asking the congregation to stand as God had me give the benediction.

My response to her comment had I ever sat up front in your church or ever went to the pulpit without permission, and she said no. But she said if the elder did not want to stand, I should not have disrespected him to ask him to stand. I told her to take it up with God because I only said what God asked me to say. I also informed her that I went to God and asked Him to release me from her church, and He did. She only carried out the request I brought to God.

Strength in Persecutions

My strength comes from my Abba Father; for God is our refuge and strength, a very present help in trouble, Psalm 46:1 (KJV). Often, circumstances and situations may present with unfavorable conditions that appear to result in afflictions and persecutions. As I reflect on my life journey so far, I've realized that the persecutions I've endured have contributed positively to my spiritual, emotional, and mental health. This has given me such strengths and compassion and allowed me to expand my talents, gifts, callings, careers, and creativity. I have set standards, developed skills, values, and morals, and developed a zero-tolerance for abuse, disrespect, and leaders' abuse of their authority. I have viewed how the persecutions I endured and the delays were opportunities to strengthen my relationship with God and others.

I have learned to identify what works and what doesn't. I continue to determine what needs changing and what to leave alone because change is not forthcoming. I have many passions; I continue to identify ways to help others with my time, resources, skills, talents, intercessory prayers, and services to many community members.

I USUALLY DO when I have identified ways and situations that I can act, and I am very conscious about how I can impact situations, processes, relationships, and the better good of people.

God shuts and opens doors. Doors are open for us to walk through. In life, we must discern the seasons and times, and when God closes doors, we must understand that they are to stay closed. God removes people and things we should never reconnect to from our lives. God is the Alpha and the Omega; He knows the beginning from the end and what's in between. When God told Abraham to leave his family and country of origin, God said to go from the familiar because God had something better for him.

Many Questions for You to Reflect

Has God shut any door in your life? _____
_____
_____
_____
_____

Has God sent you out of your birthplace? _____
_____
_____
_____
_____

Has God moved you from among your family? _____
_____
_____
_____
_____

Have you ever experienced living in a strange place? _____
_____
_____
_____
_____

How did you feel having to trust God in all things? _____
_____
_____

_____

_____

What advice do you have for anyone experiencing struggles in his/her
life? _____

_____

_____

_____

_____

Are you a college graduate? _____

_____

_____

_____

_____

What does it feel like to raise your children alone? _____

_____

_____

_____

_____

What would you do if you are jobless and must care for your minor
children? _____

_____

_____

_____

_____

How would you care for your family when no government assistance is
available? _____

_____

_____

_____

_____

Did you grow up with extended family living with you or strangers
living among you? _____

_____

_____

_____

_____

What is/was your relationship with your grandmother? _____

_____

_____

_____

_____

What is/was your relationship with your mother? _____

_____

_____

_____

_____

How is/was your relationship with your father? _____

_____

_____

_____

_____

Have you ever felt uneasy amongst family or friend? _____

_____

_____

_____

_____

What was your sleeping arrangement as a child? _____

_____

_____

_____

_____

Did you have to share a bed or room with anyone? _____

_____

_____

_____

_____

Have you experienced any abuse? _____

_____

_____

_____

_____

Were you sexually abuse? _____ What age? _____ What happened? ____

_____

_____

_____

_____

What have you done after you were sexually abused or rape? _____

_____

_____

_____

_____

Who would you trust to share the sexually abuse with? _____

_____

_____

_____

_____

Why would you trust this person? _____

_____

_____

_____

_____

What would you do if you were told to keep your mouth shut about the rape or sexual abuse? _____

_____

_____

_____

_____

How do you qualify a person to walk with you? _____

_____

_____

_____

_____

Affliction of Abuse of my Vessel

Quotation: *When our purpose is unknown our destiny is unknown by Gurmay Effrige Fraser*

Before moving in with Giver and Ralph, her partner, my chores shifted and increased many times. Sometimes it felt like I was the only child living in the household. The other children always seemed to have time and fun playing with friends and relaxing, while I was always called to do other chores left undone by my family members. Even though this was bothersome, I felt needed and less neglected by my grandmother.

On the other hand, my mother, her partner, and my siblings lived in their new environment and continued to stabilize their living situation. I saw my mother sporadically during her visits to my grandmother or either during church services or community events.

My feelings about my grandmother's feelings towards me did not shift any, and I continued to feel that she tolerated my presence but did not welcome me living in her home. I began to feel an emotional disconnect between my grandmother and myself. It was hard to explain, but what I noticed was when I spoke with my grandmother, even though she would be either sitting or standing next to me, she seemed distant and was no longer emotionally available or emotionally connected to what I was saying. I would have so much to say to her, but she would insist that I shut my mouth, and if I didn't, she would warn me that she would spank me for disobedience. These times were the beginning of hearing others, including my grandmother, calling me or referring to me by many names instead of my birth name.

The Afflictions of the Righteous

So many times, I was called by names that were not my name, and when I heard these names even at a young age, I was provoked, and it made me angry, but I couldn't explain why when I was called outside my name, I felt angry. During those times, I did not realize that this was emotional abuse. When I was called these derogatory names, it always made me feel less like a person. I was four years old and months, but even at that young age, I felt bad about myself, and I felt something was wrong with me because if nothing were wrong, then some of my family would not call me names that made me feel ashamed, inferior to others, and belittle among other feelings.

Psychological/Emotional Abuse

I had problems with poor social skills and became withdrawn and shy. I hated speaking, especially in front of people and had attention deficit problems with inattentiveness, but I enjoyed daydreaming. I remembered that I was always so shy and afraid to speak or speak up for fear of getting into trouble for saying the wrong things. I felt that if I stayed quiet, I would stay out of trouble, and I would not have to hear my family calling me nasty names. I remember when I was called so many disrespectful names, it would hurt me so badly that I would feel the pain as if it was a physical assault on me. Then I would cry, which is when it got worse because now cry baby was a name added to their list of names. I was called many names, such as an ugly red girl, red Ackery (this is a fish), dummy, dunce, stupid, good for nothing, comments that you will never amount to anything good, shut up, skinny, foolish… I was isolated from the family, especially during the months I slept on that cold concrete living room floor next to the rapist Young.

I dreaded coming home from school, let alone going to bed. Sometimes I would sneak into the bedroom with my sheet and lie on the floor, only to be found by my grandmother, who would send me back to the living room floor where rapist Young was always waiting. I became distracted in school and isolated at home and in the community. I often wondered when my mother was coming to get me. I became withdrawn, isolated, and mistrustful of adults. I did poorly in school in all areas of academics because of the poison and now the sexual abuse.

When I refused to comply, I was sent to either stand in a corner facing the wall or kneeled facing the corner of a wall for many hours. Sometimes I fell asleep facing the wall while kneeling or standing, and I couldn't tell how long I was there. If I dared turn to look to see what was happening and I got caught, my time in the corner was extended, and I might get a beating with a cane or whatsoever was close by.

Physical Abuse

I cannot remember how many beatings I've received and how many times I was beaten for things I didn't do. I was always the go-to person if anything was wrong because I had done it. Even if I were asked if I had anything to do with the violation, as I was opening my mouth to share or say anything, I was commanded to "shut up," and then the rod of correction, a cane, was used to hit me anywhere on my body that the cane struck. During this era, beating children was the norm; sometimes, the blows would leave bloody marks on my body. My skin would be bruised and swollen for days, and it would be painful to wash my body or put on certain clothing. Whenever I would be called to receive a beating, as much as I did not want it, I would become terrified of not going because it was always worse if I refused. Using objects nearby was the norm, and these objects like a leather belt that was soaked in water, shoes, pots, punching, hitting, slaps, physical restraint, threatening to repeat the physical restraint, or missing a meal were very normal.

Sexual Abuse

My sleeping arrangement remained on the concrete living room floor. The floor was cold and had no carpet or padding or floor covering. As I continued to sleep on the living room floor, rapist Young joined his bed on the floor next to my bed. The floor would become colder at night, and in the early morning, I would feel the cold on the thin bed sheet I laid on. My grandmother did not attempt to put comforters or blankets to pad the concrete floor for me to sleep on. Instead, she complained that she didn't want me wetting her sheets. I never understood why I was forced to share a floor as a sleeping arrangement with a grown man, and I was allowed to endanger my life. I was raped repeatedly, and this was swept under the carpet. I remember when I approached my grandmother, letting her know that I was inappropriately touched and was raped. Instead of her investigating the incident, I got a hit in the mouth for letting secrets out, and my grandmother responded by calling me a liar. Grandmother said that I was accused of lying to this God-fearing man.

I was also told that nobody wanted me anyway, and I would have nowhere to live, especially since my mother's partner took her with five children that are not his. I was told my mother's partner sure didn't want me because I was one of the oldest. Also, I was told that if my grandmother threw me, I was not allowed to return to my grandmother's house. I was told that I was not thankful for a place to stay. I became obedient to the directions of my grandmother and listened to her.

I was again told that I could only sleep on the living room floor. I continued to sleep on the cold concrete floor, and rapist Young continued sexually abusing me. I physically fought the rapist, but some nights I had no strength to fight this grown man rapist. I hated nights because I was afraid to go to sleep, and when I did dose off to sleep, I would be awakened by being sexually abused. I would also hate the dark because when I would become awakened by being sexually abused, it was always pitch dark, and it caused me to become trapped by rapist Young. I had more of a struggle fighting him to get free as I struggled to process which way to escape from him, and of course, I never did because he used his body to trap me by laying on top of me, and me having felt suffocated

The information and resources below are from betterhelp. com. If ever you feel that you are being abused either emotional or psychological, physically or sexually, please know that you can become proactive by following the steps below:

Have a Safety Plan

Step 1: Get Help Early

What are the warning signs that you are beginning to struggle with your problem? These can include thoughts, feelings, or behaviors or eating or sleeping: _____

_____

_____

_____

_____

Step 2: How do you Cope

What do you do to take your mind off your problems? Are there obstacles that would prevent you to use these coping skills? _____

_____

_____

_____

_____

Step 3: Establish Your Social Support NETWORK

When you feel distress contact your trusted family members, friends, neighbors, co-workers, classmates, medical professionals, church families, tribe. List several people in case your first choices are unavailable. _____

_____

_____

_____

_____

Name: _____

Contact Info: _____

Name: _____

Contact Info: _____

Name: _____

Contact Info: _____

Step 4: Seek Help from Professionals

If your problem persists, or if you have suicidal thoughts, reach out to your professional support system.

Local emergency number: _____

Professional or agency: _____

In the United States

Emergency: 911
National Domestic Violence Hotline: 1- 800-799-7233
National Suicide Prevention Lifeline: 1-800-273-TALK (8255)
National Hope line Network: 1-800-SUICIDE (800-784-2433)
Crisis Text Line: Text "DESERVE" TO 741-741
Lifeline Crisis Chat (Online live messaging):
https://suicidepreventionlifeline.org/chat/
Self-Harm Hotline: 1-800-DONT CUT (1-800-366-8288)
Essential local and community services: 211, https://www.211.org/
Planned Parenthood Hotline: 1-800-230-PLAN (7526)
American Association of Poison Control Centers: 1-800-222-1222
National Council on Alcoholism & Drug Dependency Hope
Line: 1-800-622-2255
National Crisis Line - Anorexia and Bulimia: 1-800-233-4357
GLBT Hotline: 1-888-843-4564
TREVOR Crisis Hotline: 1-866-488-7386
AIDS Crisis Line: 1-800-221-7044
Veterans Crisis Line: https://www.veteranscrisisline.net
TransLifeline: https://www.translifeline.org - 877-565-8860
Suicide Prevention Wiki: http://suicideprevention.wikia.com

UK & Republic of Ireland

Emergency: 112 or 999
Non-emergency: 111, Option 2
24/7 Helpline: 116 123 (UK and ROI)
Shout: Text "DESERVE" TO 85258
Samaritans.org: https://www.samaritans.org/how-we-can-help-you/
contact-us
YourLifeCounts.org: https://yourlifecounts.org/find-help/

Argentina

Emergency: 911
Argentina Suicide Hotline: +5402234930430

Spain

Emergency: 112
Telefono De La Esperanza - 717-003-717 - http://
telefonodelaesperanza.org/llamanos

Australia

Emergency: 000
Lifeline.org: https://www.lifeline.org.au/Get-Help/Online-Services/
crisis-chat
Lifeline Australia: 1-300-13-11-14
YourLifeCounts.org: https://yourlifecounts.org/find-help/
Beyond Blue https://www.beyondblue.org.au/get-support/get-
immediate-support

China

Emergency 110
Beijing Suicide Research and Prevention Center http://www.crisis.
org.cn/ 800-810-1117 (landline) or 010-8295-1332 (mobile and
VoIP callers)
Shanghai Mental Health Center http://www.smhc.org.cn/
Lifeline Shanghai https://www.lifeline-shanghai.com/

Canada

Emergency: 911
Crisis Text Line (Powered by Kids Help Phone):
Text "DESERVE" TO 686868
YourLifeCounts.org: https://yourlifecounts.org/find-help/
Crisis Services Canada: http://www.crisisservicescanada.ca/en/
Canadian Association for Suicide Prevention: https://
suicideprevention.ca/need-help/

South Africa

Emergency: 10 111 for police or 10 177 for an ambulance
24hr Helpline: 0800 12 13 14 or SMS 31393
Depression and Anxiety Helpline: 0800 70 80 90
YourLifeCounts.org: https://yourlifecounts.org/find-help/

New Zealand

Emergency: 111
Lifeline 24/7 Helpline: 0800 543 354
Suicide Crisis Helpline: 0508 828 865 (0508 TAUTOKO)
YourLifeCounts.org: https://yourlifecounts.org/find-help/

India

Emergency: 112
Sneha India (http://www.snehaindia.org) is available 24/7 on the phone by calling 91 44 24640050

Germany

Emergency: 112
Hotline: 800 111 0111
Hotline: 0800 111 0222
YourLifeCounts.org: https://yourlifecounts.org/find-help/

Finland

Emergency: 112
Crisis Line: 010 195 202

Argentina

Emergency: 911
Argentina Suicide Hotline: +5402234930430

Spain

Emergency: 112
Telefono De La Esperanza - 717-003-717
http://telefonodelaesperanza.org/llamanos

Australia

Emergency: 000
Lifeline.org: https://www.lifeline.org.au/Get-Help/Online-Services/crisis-chat
Life Line Australia: 1-300-13-11-14

YourLifeCounts.org: https://yourlifecounts.org/find-help/
Beyond Blue https://www.beyondblue.org.au/get-support/get-immediate-support

China

Emergency 110
Beijing Suicide Research and Prevention Center http://www.crisis.org.cn/ 800-810-1117 (landline) or 010-8295-1332 (mobile and VoIP callers)
Shanghai Mental Health Center http://www.smhc.org.cn/
Lifeline Shanghai https://www.lifeline-shanghai.com/

Canada

Emergency: 911
Crisis Text Line (Powered by Kids Help Phone): Text "DESERVE" TO 686868
YourLifeCounts.org: https://yourlifecounts.org/find-help/
Crisis Services Canada: http://www.crisisservicescanada.ca/en/
Canadian Association for Suicide Prevention: https://suicideprevention.ca/need-help/

South Africa

Emergency: 10 111 for police or 10 177 for an ambulance
24hr Helpline: 0800 12 13 14 or SMS 31393
Depression and Anxiety Helpline: 0800 70 80 90
YourLifeCounts.org: https://yourlifecounts.org/find-help/

New Zealand

Emergency: 111
Lifeline 24/7 Helpline: 0800 543 354
Suicide Crisis Helpline: 0508 828 865 (0508 TAUTOKO)
YourLifeCounts.org: https://yourlifecounts.org/find-help/

India

Emergency: 112
Sneha India (http://www.snehaindia.org) is available 24/7 on the phone by calling 91 44 24640050

Germany

Emergency: 112
Hotline: 800 111 0111
Hotline: 0800 111 0222
YourLifeCounts.org: https://yourlifecounts.org/find-help/

Finland

Emergency: 112
Crisis Line: 010 195 202

Facing the Giants in my Life That Fell and Died

The sexual abuse at that time for those incidents ended when I relocated to live with my mother, her partner, and my siblings. Their home was a few miles from my school. There was no transportation in my family, school, or city bus to transport me to and from school. Therefore, I walked more than four miles to school round trip daily. I walked to school in the morning, then back home for lunch, then back to school after lunch, and then back home at the end of the day.

Lateness was not accepted; I had to be on time. If I were late, the school doors were locked until after prayer was done. Then after prayers, the headmistress or headmaster would approach me with a cane, and I would be beaten on my legs, back, and arms and wherever else the lashes would register. At one time in my life, I had no shoes -- therefore, I walked barefoot to and from school. In Guyana, South America, the weather was tropical year-round, and the temperature was usually over eighty degrees daily. Rain may frequently fall during the day, and then the sun would come out; sometimes, it would rain while the sun was shining. I challenge anyone to walk on the street with the bricks and stones heated beyond eighty degrees; this is very hot. Sometimes I would have to run to school because of the ground heat as I walked barefooted.

In those days, I wrote on a black slate with white chalk; composition books and paper were available to the rich students whose parents could afford to purchase these. My home had no running water, electricity, telephone, and gas stove; it had no refrigerator or ice box, appliances, and carpets. Daily, my siblings and I were required to fetch water from the creek about two miles round trip before going to school to fill the water barrel. The bathroom and toilet were outdoors, away from the house, and my family and I and our neighbors nearby shared these facilities. I slept on a mattress on the floor and then eventually shared a bed and bedroom. My family moved into the country to a big frame house in which my grandmother and her family had previously lived.

I remembered distinctly that it was a Sunday. I had dressed up under the dining room table with a cloth as a blind (curtain) and pieces of wood I made into furniture and had it like a doll house. Another family friend, Mr. Happy, came to visit and began to talk to Giver, my mother. He then came to the dining room area where I was playing with my dolls under the table and began talking to me.

When is it ever enough?

The next moment, I saw and felt his hand on my body, and he immediately touched my private part inappropriately. I took the Carnation milk can I had in my doll house and threw it at him, hitting him hard on his forehead. His forehead was immediately swollen. He began to scream and yell that I was a crazy girl and would amount to nothing good. My mother never asked what happened but began to advance toward me with a belt, and I ran outside away from my mother and stayed there. My mother yelled, "Your father (my mother's partner, Ralph) will deal with it when he gets home from work!"

Use What You Got, my Teeth to Bite

However, when Ralph came in from work, Giver reported the incident to him, and he called me, and I came when he called my name. He did not ask me what happened, but he picked me up and immediately began to beat me. I began to fight him to get loose from his grip as I yelled that Mr. Happy was touching my private part. My mother's partner continued to beat me, and because he refused to stop beating me or listen to me, I bit him so hard on his free hand, and I continued to bite him until he let me loose. He eventually let me loose, as he was in pain. That was the first, and the last time I was beaten by my mother's partner, Ralph. I made an oath that I was going to protect myself regardless of the cost. I had no intention of biting him, but then again, he didn't understand, nor did he want to understand that this so-called family friend, Happy, was sexually molesting me; nor was he aware that I had been previously sexually raped, either. I did not feel comfortable with this challenge of having to appear that I was disrespecting my mother's partner; however, I had to stand up to stop the abuse and ignite my faith to know that I might be likely to receive a beating, but the stronghold must be destroyed to overcome the early challenges and abuse I've endured when I had no one to protect me even when they were aware.

I had many challenges and tribulations in my life, some to process through and others to overcome. I had severe learning problems. While sitting in the classroom, I often daydreamed and had many wonderful visions that eased the pain of my life's giants. Many times, while I was in class in school, I felt like these teachers were speaking foreign languages because I had no comprehension of what the teachers were saying, so I was unable to process what was being said. I could not write what the teachers said because I couldn't spell words or do the assignments that the teachers gave. I often scribbled on paper to make it appear as though I was taking notes. However, when the teachers came around and checked the students' work, they found that my writing was gibberish, and this made the teachers angry. I became a target, and from then on, I was frequently called to answer questions I did not know how to answer.

These behaviors that I displayed, according to my teachers, warranted beatings in front of my peers in my classes. Beatings were done with bamboo sticks, and the lashes went all over my body: my back, arms, legs, shoulders, and wherever else the lashes went because I moved while these lashes were inflicted. My peers frequently laughed at me, made fun, and called me names like a dummy, dunce, and stupid. Some of my peers refused to be seen in public, close to me, or be in my presence. I began to feel that these names were correct because I just could not perform academically in school and that whatever I had that caused my brain not to be smart like the other kids might be contagious. That was why my peers refused to be in my company. My peers would whisper around me, and it appeared they always had something going on. I was never invited to their homes, parties, or dances. I was called the "ugly duckling," and some of my peers would follow with "quack, quack," while others would make the sign with their hands. This caused me to become very withdrawn, shy, and isolated at school to the point that I would slouch in my seat, hoping not to be seen or called by teachers to answer any question and/or asked to speak.

When teachers called my name, I would panic, sweat, become nervous, and be tongue-tied, and this would cause my words to become jumbled up. This made me even more very shy and quiet. I continued to receive many beatings in school for incomplete work, lack of participation, and poor academic and social performances. This continued for many years, from kindergarten to the tenth grade of high school in Guyana, South America.

Have you experience prejudice, abuse, being bullied? Were you the abuser, were you the racist, or the bully? Why? _____

_____

_____

_____

_____

Have you been abused at school? _____

_____

_____

_____

_____

Do you know of anyone that has been beaten at school by teachers or peers? _____

_____

_____

_____

_____

Should they have been beaten? _____

_____

_____

_____

_____

Do you consider spanking from teachers' child abuse? _____

_____

_____

_____

_____

What would you have done if you were spank for coming to school late, or were academically slow? _____

_____

_____

_____

_____

How would you react if your teachers spank you for incomplete work?

_____

_____

_____

_____

_____

Do you believe that you experience poverty as a child? _____

_____

_____

_____

_____

What does poverty mean to you? _____

_____

_____

_____

_____

If you had to walk to school barefoot, what would you have done?

_____

_____

_____

_____

_____

What was your home environment like as a child? _____

_____

_____

_____

_____

Did you have running water in your home, where did you get water from? _____

_____
_____
_____

Did you have electricity? _____
_____
_____
_____

How would you have survived living in a home without refrigerator?
_____
_____
_____

What would you have done if someone called you disrespectful names?
_____
_____
_____

Have you ever received a spanking for something that you didn't do?
_____
_____
_____

What would you have done if someone touched your private parts? __
_____
_____
_____

What was the biggest challenge that you've overcome at a young age?
_____
_____

_____

_____

_____

Have you suffered physical abuse by any of your teachers? _____

_____

_____

_____

How would you react if you were emotional abuse by your teachers?

_____

_____

_____

_____

Have your teachers ever beaten you with objects? _____

_____

_____

_____

Would you consider physical beatings by teachers' abuse? _____

_____

_____

_____

Did your peers bully you? _____

_____

_____

_____

Have you ever felt isolated at school? _____

_____

_____

_____

What would you have done if your peers bullied you? _____

_____

_____

_____

_____

God's Plan is Still Inevitable Even in Broken Promises

I experienced several broken promises with my biological father, who was very good at empty promises; of all the promises he had made to me, he has not fulfilled even one. I felt that maybe he did not realize that he needed to follow through. My father's behavior started very early in my life; he could not be responsible. I know that he did love me but was unable to be in my life since he was trying to find his life, purpose, and plan God had for him. My father was also the first man in my life, and the way that he touched me, hugged me, spoke to me, and looked at me, I knew that he adored me and loved me.

Be Strong and be of Good Courage

Even though I was a young child at that time, I was able to discern good touch from bad touch. However, I felt that anyone who drank as much as my father did was looking on the outside for something he thought he had lost, not realizing that everything he ever needed for his life journey was already placed inside of him by the Abba Father. My father needed assistance to execute his purpose to fulfill his life, to bring out the gifts locked up in his womb that God had already placed in him. Instead of spending his life looking on the outside, he needed to seek God first, and God's righteousness and everything in him would have then manifested. My father made promises to me when I was only two years old while struggling to find his purpose in life. He could never fulfill any of these promises he made to me.

The next time I saw my father, I was about seven to eight years old and living in the country Matthews Ridge in the Northwest Region, in Guyana, South America. On my way home from school, my father approached me and said, "are you Gurmay?" he continued by saying, "you look like my daughter, Gurmay." So shameful he didn't even know if it were me. I looked up at him and was hesitant and scared, wondering why this stranger would be asking me questions. The last time I saw my father, I was two years old when he told me that he was going to the store to buy me candy, and I never looked at him again. Could this be him? Did he finally return with the candy about five years later? He continued to ask me questions about my family. I was so terrified when I heard him call my name, because I did not recognize him.

Courage to be Different

Therefore, I ran away from him and ran all the way home and told my mother this man had called my name and was asking me questions on the way home from school. This caused my mother to panic because my mother knew who he was. My mother was unsure of his intent to show up in the country since they had never lived there, and she wondered what his purpose was after all these years. John, my father, left, and I never knew when he did. I just never saw him again in Matthews Ridge, and I never asked Giver about him, and she never mentioned him.

Praise Instead of a spirit of Anguish

The next time I saw my father was the day before my sixteenth birthday. I lived in Georgetown, Guyana, in Agricola Village on the East Bank. I would not have recognized him if my oldest sister had not been at home when he appeared. He showed up at my home there and said that he missed me. He then gave my sister sixty dollars to shop for party food and to prepare food for my birthday the next day. He said that we would celebrate our birthdays tomorrow. I don't know how I felt. Should I be happy or sad or expect that he would show up this time. My sister went shopping for all the party foods and even invited the neighborhood children to my impromptu birthday party the next day. I have never had my birthday kept up ever before this time. I wanted to believe that the next day, my sixteen birthday to be the best because my father and I had the same birthday month and day, and yes, he promised that he would be here for us to celebrate our birthday together. This birthday, my sixteen, was supposed to be a great one since my father was going to be there.

My mother was already living in America for years, and I truly missed her. Of course, the day of my sixteen-birthday arrived, and all the guests showed up. My home was nicely decorated, and the party foods and fluids were displayed. The music was playing, and everyone, including myself, waited and waited. I began to feel uneasy, and the feelings increased to panic and anxiety. We kept waiting until it darkened, and he never showed up. I was so embarrassed. I couldn't even eat, and many times I had to leave the room to cry and compose myself, and I never heard from nor saw him until many years later.

The next time I saw my father, John, I was 24 years old with my firstborn on vacation in Guyana, South America. John showed up, and this time I recognized him. He wanted to know what I had brought for him, and he introduced himself to my daughter as her grandfather and stretched his hands towards my daughter. My daughter clung to me, hid her face in my bosom, and kept asking me who this strange man was. I never told my daughter about John because I blocked him out of my life, and I was now living in a new country, and I didn't want my daughter to endure the pain I did by waiting for John to show he never did. At that moment, though, I mentioned to my daughter that John is my father, but he has not been in my life, neither has he kept any promises he made to me nor visited as promised.

While in Guyana, I saw him a few times on that visit and gave him money, bought him food, and shared gifts with him. He then disappeared and again never visited, neither did I know where he lives with his recent wife. Again, he went missing, and when I enquired from my family about his whereabouts, no one knew where he was. I left Guyana, South America, and I did not see nor hear from him before I left.

Another broken promise that disappointed me was when my best friend, my fifth sibling, my brother John, jr., was murdered by the Death Squad, a branch of the Guyana Police Force whose motto is "Shoot first and ask questions later." His death was a shock. It's only through the mercy and grace of God upon my life that I did not end up where I would not mention. I had spoken to my brother shortly before he was murdered, and we promised to see each other soon. The next time I saw him, he was in a coffin.

His death caused me to take life very seriously because, until this time, I had not experienced such a tragedy as murder. Why does a system that is supposed to protect its citizens murder an innocent person who was harmless while the Government does nothing to bring justice or hold their people responsible? It took me a long time to recover from this trauma. Since this trauma, I have not returned to my native country. I believe that if I did not have God's grace and mercy and my children, it is impossible to know what would have become of me. During this time, I was a full-time student attending Adelphi University, Medgar Evers College, and simultaneously working full-time as an assistant teacher.

Just as I began to smile again and relax, another tragedy struck. My other best friend, my oldest sibling, and my sister died in childbirth in Atlanta, Georgia, shortly before graduating with her nursing degree. I had spoken to my oldest sister the day after my birthday, and she agreed to attend my birthday party set for the following weekend. I was in a business meeting when I received a disturbing phone call. This phone call came two days before my sister arrived in New York for my birthday party. Instead of celebrating, I was now making arrangements to travel South to Georgia. As I traveled to the hospital, I felt that I was dreaming and would soon wake up because that usually happens when someone dreams. My dream ended at the hospital when the reality of the crisis was staring me in the face. I looked at my best friend, my older sister, as she lay there with tubes and machines attached to her body and running from all directions. As I stood, dumbfounded and in shock, unable to grasp and comprehend what I was looking at, I walked toward my sister and simply hugged her as I prayed to my Heavenly Father God. My sister and I made plans to always be friends and support each other regardless of our situations.... another broken promise, and no one could say how. For years I felt disappointed by my oldest sister's death.

I became angry – and even worse, lonely -- and very disappointed with life. My sister promised always to be there for me and me for her. Oh, how I loved my sister. I always was reassured that my sister would fix whatever was broken in my life. This sister was my only confidante during those lonely years of my sexual abuse and rape; growing up without a mother and father; being teased because I was not able to read and write; also during the years of trials and tribulations that I endured while living in America with my two siblings that came with my mother years before I came to America. I remembered that my eldest sister would be so excited when Friday came around because I would pack my children's bags, go to my sister's apartment, and spend almost every weekend with her and her family.

My oldest sister was the only one that stood up to our grandmother, Maria, about my sexual abuse and rape when I confronted my grandmother while in America, as my grandmother tried to deny that I ever told her about the sexual abuse and rape. This sister was also sexually abused when she was sent to take food to one of the men our grandmother cooked for, Mr. Jim, who was also having a relationship with our grandmother. I remember on one occasion when I accompanied my sister to take food, Jim did not know that I was there outside waiting for my sister. When we got to his house, the door was closed but unlocked, and when my sister knocked on the door, he told her to come in. He then called her into the bedroom, where he was to give her a candy (a sweetie) as she gave him the food in his bedroom. She was obedient because we were taught to respect our elders, no matter what. Anyhow, I realized that my sister was staying in the bedroom too long, and I pushed the door open and went to the bedroom, and I saw him trying to pull the clothes off my sister as she tried to fight him off. I picked up an object, advanced toward him, and ordered him to let her go. After that, I never allowed my sister to go to drop off food without accompanying her. Our relationship was inseparable.

Years later, I had knee surgery. That same week my sister and family relocated to Georgia. I saw her once after this. I missed her so much and was so lost without her that I traveled to Georgia and made up for lost time with her. The second time I saw my sister, she was on her deathbed. As my sister's medical reality came flooding back to me, I was now confronted with the present moment. Her baby was in her fallopian tube for the second time, and this time after surgery was performed, she slipped into a coma and never came out.

At her bedside in the hospital, I began to pray over my sister; I spoke to her and commanded my sister to squeeze my hand if she could hear me because I knew she could hear me. My sister not only squeezed my hand but also cried, and I saw tears rolling down her eyes. I said to my sister that last week on the phone, we promised to meet up but not this way. She was supposed to meet me in New York for my birthday celebration. This would have been the second time my birthday was kept up, and this was my fortieth birthday. I began to bargain with my sister telling her that it was not fair that she was not honoring her agreement to be there for each other. I told my sister that she needed to fight to get out of her space. The tears continued to roll down her face.

My sister was waiting for my appearance at the hospital. When I left the hospital around 3:00 am, my sister died within hours, and she went to meet the Lord. When someone you have known all your life, who stood in the gap as a surrogate mother, who was always there for you... was there with you to wipe every tear of disappointment, to laugh with you at every achievement, and was always there to comfort all your fears and to tell you that you will be just fine -- and suddenly you wake up to find that this person is no longer there nor is she ever returning because God had another assignment for her life ... how does someone continue to live with such intolerable loss and pain? Now Faith is the substance of things hoped for, the evidence of things not seen, Hebrews 11:1 (KJV). How would I continue when the only person I could confide in and who knew everything about me was gone permanently? How would I endure during the years of uncertainty? Only God, my Abba Father.

How would you Process or Handle any of the situations below?

When you were little, have you experienced any broken promises from your parents? _____

_____

_____

_____

_____

Which parent? _____

_____

_____

_____

_____

What were those broken promises? _____

_____

_____

_____

_____

How did this make you feel? _____

_____

_____

_____

_____

Were you able to let your parent (s) know how you felt? _____

_____

_____

_____

_____

Was your parent (s) involved in any substance abuse? _____

_____

_____

_____

_____

What about infidelity? _____

_____

_____

_____

_____

Were they any children birthed out of the adulterous relationship?

_____

_____

_____

_____

Has this affected your relationship with your parent (s) later in life? __

_____

_____

_____

_____

_____

What do you do to prevent you from repeating these behaviors to your children? _____

_____

_____

_____

_____

Do you know of anyone whose parent (s) was not involved in his/her life? _____

_____

_____

_____

_____

How do you feel about parents that are irresponsible? _____

_____

_____

_____

_____

Would you call the man that raise you your daddy, if he was not your biological father? _____

_____

_____

_____

_____

Are you a responsible person or parent? _____

_____

_____

_____

_____

Are you married? _____

_____

_____

_____

Are you faithful to yourself and your spouse? _____

_____

_____

_____

How do you feel about parents that are unfaithful to their marriage and relationship? _____

_____

_____

_____

What would you do if you found out that your spouse is unfaithful?

_____

_____

_____

_____

Do you believe in staying in a relationship if your spouse is unfaithful once or more than once? _____

_____

_____

_____

Using words, how would you describe your relationship with your spouse? _____

_____

_____

_____

If I were to ask your son/daughter about your responsibility as a parent, what would they say? _____

_____

_____

_____

_____

How do you know if your parent loves you? _____

_____

_____

_____

_____

How does your parent show you that they love you? _____

_____

_____

_____

_____

Do you love yourself, child/children? _____

_____

_____

_____

_____

How do you show your child/children that you love them? _____

_____

_____

_____

_____

What will you do differently from your parent (s)? _____

_____

_____

_____

_____

How do you emotionally engage in your children's life? _____

_____

_____

_____

_____

How are you involved in your children's school? _____

_____

_____

_____

_____

Who is your support or network for childcare? _____

_____

_____

_____

_____

Do you have a backup assistance to help you with childcare? _____

_____

_____

_____

_____

How do you qualify people to provide childcare? _____

_____

_____

_____

_____

Do you know what God's plan and purpose is for your life? _____

_____

_____

_____

_____

Have you experienced any broken promises at a young age or as a
teenager? _____

_____

_____

_____

What about broken promises as an adult? _____

_____

_____

_____

_____

How many times have you experienced broken promises? _____

_____

_____

_____

_____

Have you ever lost anyone that you were close with? _____

_____

_____

_____

_____

How would you describe that relationship? _____

_____

_____

_____

_____

How did that person make you feel? _____

_____

_____

_____

_____

How did you cope with that lost? _____

_____

_____

_____

_____

What was the worse trauma that you have experienced with broken promises? _____

_____

_____

_____

_____

Have you recovered? _____

_____

_____

_____

_____

How long did it take you to recover? _____

_____

_____

_____

_____

What did you do to recover? _____

_____

_____

_____

_____

Has any of your love one's ever been murdered? _____

_____

_____

_____

_____

How did this happen? _____

_____

_____

_____

_____

How were you comforted during the time of grieving? _____

_____

_____

_____

_____

Who comforted you? _____

_____

_____

_____

_____

How do you handle traumatic situations? _____

_____

_____

_____

_____

How do you feel about broken promises? _____

_____

_____

_____

_____

Have you ever witnessed anyone being raped? _____

_____

_____

_____

_____

Have you ever stopped someone from being raped? _____

_____

_____

_____

_____

What would you do if you saw someone being raped? _____

_____

_____

_____

_____

Endurance during the Years of Uncertainty

Quotation: *When sight is invisible our vision is inevitable by Gurmay Effrige Fraser*

These were the events of the summer of 1975 when I was sixteen; I could never forget them even if I wanted to. The last summer vacation before I came to the United States of America. I revisited Matthews Ridge with my maternal aunt, Olivia, and stayed with my maternal grandmother, Maria. I was nervous, anxious and at the same time excited about going back to the same place and my maternal grandmother, Maria's home. Because it was at this very location, Guyana, South America, in Matthews Ridge in the Northwest Region and with this very person Maria when I live with her that I was raped repeatedly at four years old, this time my logic was I'm no longer four years old I am 16 years eight months old, and I can take care of myself because I'm now 115 pounds, 5 feet 5 inches and stronger and wiser. So, I accepted Olivia's offer to revisit Matthews Ridge to reconnect, bask in the environment, enjoy the countryside, and the delicious fruits, visit family I've not seen in years, and most importantly, put the rape behind me, or so I thought.

On Monday afternoon, I traveled from Georgetown by the Lady North Court boat, and it docked at Morawhanna. Then we took a smaller boat to Port Kaituma, then got on a train to Matthews Ridge, where we got a car ride to Maria's home. This time she no longer lived in the building and shared the home with another tenant; she had her own frame home located down a hill and below the only police station. I walked on the narrow bridge with my plastic shopping bags containing my belongings and up the many stairs to her front door.

The last time I saw Maria was many years ago, and I was hesitant to see her again because the few times she visited Agricola Village, where I lived, she was never approachable. I always felt that I was walking on eggshells around her. I don't ever recall her calling me by my name, Gurmay Effrige. I'm named after her, and her name was Gurmay Effrige Maria.

The door was opened, so I knocked on it so that she would know I was there before entering. Maria was sitting in her big chair made of cane material and smoking a cigarette. She looked up at me and did not utter a word nor get up to embrace or greet me. Immediately I felt this cold vibration go through my body, and I stood there in unbelieve, numbness, and shock. I did not know if I should advance toward her or allow her to get out of the chair and come toward me, or I should go toward her. I stood there frozen for what seemed like an eternity. I began to feel like a stranger that showed up, and my appearance felt uninvited and unwelcome. Finally, I spoke and said, hello, Sister Maria. She hated and forbade me to call her grandma or grandmother. She then nodded, and then I said that auntie Olivia brought me to visit the countryside of Matthews Ridge before I traveled to the United States of America. Auntie Olivia said that I could stay here with you while I was here on vacation. When Maria finally spoke, she said, "I guess I will have to share my bed with you," so go put your bags in my room as she pointed to the first room in the house. I went to the room's door, and there was a custom-built bed, a little bigger than a twin but not big enough to be called a full-size bed.

It dawned on me that either I was not welcome there or Maria was not told I was coming to stay with her while on summer vacation. But either way, I knew I would stay out of her way. I was very uncomfortable sharing her bed, especially since she never allowed me to sleep on any bed when I was four years old, and she ordered me to sleep on that cold concrete floor and allowed me to be raped repletely by a rapist Young. I was no longer excited to be there in Matthews Ridge, and I realized that I never stopped to think of having a backup plan. God help me! I just feel very uncomfortable, unsafe, and unprotected, and I hope that history does not repeat itself. Suddenly, I feel that I'm inside the lion's den and that my life may be in danger.

I was conversing with Bert, a young man who wanted to marry me when I turned 16 years old, but he was very possessive and jealous, and I felt that I needed time from him to think. Even at age sixteen, I tried hard to be accepted by my grandmother Maria and wanted to pretend that the years of sexual abuse and rape when I was four years of age was a mistake and that Maria was sorry for allowing that to happen to me.

God Fights my Battles

Just as I got off the boat at Port Kaituma, I had a vision, and, in this vision, I saw rapist Young coming toward me and walking toward the direction where I would get on the train to take me to Matthews Ridge. In this vision, rapist Young was coming in my direction, and I could see him from a distance and looking straight at me. As he was face to face with me getting ready to pass me, he hesitated, then stopped and said, "are you Gurmay's granddaughter?" I looked him straight in his face and looked right over him and did not speak nor acknowledge his question but kept walking. I saw in the vision that he went past, stopped, and looked back.

Get Out of my Way

Less than five minutes after this vision, rapist Young approached in person in the distance. He was coming toward me, and I was walking toward him, and as we came face to face and as he passed me, he momentarily stopped and said, "are you Gurmay's granddaughter?" I looked right into his face, his eyes, and I never responded to his question, nor have I greeted him to acknowledge his presence, but I kept walking. When I looked back, sure enough, he looked back at me. After this encounter, I began to experience an anxiety attack and was hyperventilated. I had to stop and calm down before continuing my journey, walking toward the train to get on it. I never thought I would be physically confronted by a rapist Young and sexual abuser after all these years. I was on my way to having fun with my cousins, uncles, and aunts and to completely burying the years of the torment of rape and sexual molestation that occurred at Matthews Ridge.

I was also going to be in the same neighborhood with my cousin, Boyer, who had poisoned me when I was three months old, and I honestly looked at that near-death experience as an accident. I also went to the school neighborhood where I was beaten with canes because I was not learning and had severe learning deficit problems.

I was now very nervous, panicky, and unsure about this vacation. I wanted to believe that Maria did love me and that she had made a mistake by commanding me to sleep on the living room floor with this rapist man who was in his forties and raped me for several months. For many years, I felt I had to be a bad person because I was always accused of anything that happened that was bad and had to deal with the consequences. I was convinced that because I was referred to as a bad or a problem child, then it was fitting that I should be raped and abused sexually. I had to prove to myself that I was loved by Maria, my grandmother, and this rape, physical, and emotional sexual abuse was a mistake and that Maria was sorry. My aunt Olivia took me to the country, Matthews Ridge; however, she did not invite me to come to stay at her house.

At Maria's home, I felt like I was at a stranger's home that I was begging to lodge because I had no other place to stay at that time. Maria assigned me chores that first day and informed me what she expected of me while I was there. Wow! I thought this would be a fun vacation, more like a slave camp. Anyway, I went along with Maria's plan. I surely was not going to rock the boat to get thrown out and become homeless. I was far from home, and this trip was a four-day trip to arrive at Maria's location. I was expected to get out of bed at 5:00 am every morning to assist with the preparation of meal preparation and washing their flask, and sharing their breakfast with some of the same men except for Giver's partner. I had to prepare the baking pans for bread and cakes, wash dishes, and fetch water from the pipe in the yard. This was no fun at all, and I detest this arrangement.

Shortly after arrival at Maria's house, I went to visit Boyer, my cousin that pried my mouth open and poured acid down my throat when I was three months old. I thought that she would be so excited to see me. While visiting Boyer, she became angry because I refused to do something she asked me to, and I knew it was wrong. She got angry and agitated and cursed me; then, she began yelling at me and saying that I should have died when she poisoned me at three months old. She screamed that she didn't know why I was still alive.

I began to weep uncontrollably and with nowhere else to go but back to Maria's house, running from one extreme to another, not knowing which was worse since both Boyer and Maria had endangered my life at a younger age. I ran from Boyer's house and never looked back; I have never set my eyes on her. During this time at Maria's home, it was a terrible experience. If when Maria woke me up at 5:00 am each morning, and I did not get up right away, she would stomp into the bedroom and begin to speak so loudly, calling me stupid girl, good for nothing, big mouth, and she would pull the covers off me demanding I get up right away assist her with her preparation of baking bread and setting up her meals for the men. Maria never woke her children up. Almost every night Maria would leave me in this big house alone.

Bert, the man who wanted me to marry him, also showed up in Matthews Ridge at Maria's house, and she not only allowed him to spend time in the same house but welcomed him with open arms in my presence and told him he could stay as long as he wanted. Many times, Maria went out at night. I was left at the mercy of Bert, who was always around. He confronted me many times to get back as friends with me, and I refused on all occasions. He became very frustrated and advanced toward me by threatening me. He told me that if he couldn't get me, then no one else would, simply because he would not let them.

Remembering Humbling Beginnings

Until we find our purpose, we will continue to be frustrated with our life. Simultaneously, my uncle, my age, would demand that I do his laundry by hand, using a scrub board and a beater, in the yard in the hot sun. There was no washing machine or dryer. He worked but refused to provide a stipend for his laundry service. I spoke to Maria about this, but she became upset and said I was ungrateful because I refused to do my uncle's laundry. Maria said she would send me back to her mother, my great-grandmother, and Leila's home before the vacation ended. I told her she needed to do just that whenever she was ready. Maria did not change from when I lived with her when I was raped, sexually molested, and physically and emotionally abused to when I revisited her on this vacation. I felt that my life was always in turmoil, and people always expected me to allow them to abuse me. I got to the realization that I will always have to stand up against unrighteous acts and behaviors of abusers, even if this was in my family, and I refuse to tolerate people treating me in ways and action that is abusive. I know that in life, you get what you tolerate.

Your Personal Assessment and Reflections

Are you married and committed? _____

_____

_____

_____

_____

What age did you get married? _____

_____

_____

_____

_____

Is there a certain age that girls must be married? _____

_____

_____

_____

_____

How did you meet your husband? _____

_____

_____

_____

_____

Did you choose to marry your husband, or was he chosen for you?

_____

_____

_____

_____

Was or is your husband or partner jealous or abusive? _____

_____

_____

_____

_____

How did he show his jealousy? _____

_____

_____

_____

_____

How is your husband or partner abusive? _____

_____

_____

_____

_____

What would have happened if you had refused to marry your husband?

_____

_____

_____

_____

_____

Do you have family or friends that were rape? _____

_____

_____

_____

_____

Were you rape? When? What age? By Whom? _____

_____

_____

_____

_____

What advise do you have for a victim that was confronted by her rapist?

_____

_____

_____

_____

_____

How should Society treat rapist? _____
_____
_____
_____
_____

Is it justifiable that family condone rape or abuse? _____
_____
_____
_____
_____

Should family member be held legal responsible for allowing children in their care to be rape? _____
_____
_____
_____
_____

What services and programs should be mandated for rapist? _____
_____
_____
_____
_____

Did your teachers beat or abuse you? _____
_____
_____
_____
_____

How do you feel a child would react when he/she is called bad or derogatory names? _____
_____
_____
_____
_____

Were you ever called outside of your name? _____
_____
_____

_____

_____

How did this make you feel? _____

_____

_____

_____

_____

What does discipline mean to you? How were you disciplined?

_____

_____

_____

_____

_____

How did you discipline your children? _____

_____

_____

_____

_____

What advice do you have for teens that are raped? _____

_____

_____

_____

_____

Would you be able to interact with someone that attempted to murder you? _____

_____

_____

_____

_____

How did you feel about your life before age 10? _____

_____

_____

_____

_____

How did you feel about your life after age 10? _____

_____

_____

_____

_____

Were you able to share your feelings and thoughts and be heard by your parents or/and care givers? _____

_____

_____

_____

_____

Do you have any words of wisdom for someone that experienced turmoil, rejection, rape and abuse? _____

_____

_____

_____

_____

Blessings Concealed in Abusive Relationships

Quotation: *When purpose is unknown, abuse is possible by Gurmay Effrige Fraser*

Quotation: *In life, you get what you tolerate by Gurmay Effrige Fraser*

These were the continuation of the events in my life in the summer of 1975. During these times, arranged marriages were practiced, and it was customary for verbal contracts from a man's parents to a young woman's parents for their daughter to be married to their son at the daughter's set age agreed upon. Bert stated that he would marry me whether I agreed or not, and no one would stop him. He said if I refused to marry him, he would not allow any man to marry me, period.

Is this Narcissistic Personality?

Bert lived in Georgetown, Guyana, South America, in the city. Bert's parents were unmarried. Bert's father died, and his mother lives with Bert's eldest sister. Bert is twenty-two years old, weighs 168 pounds, and is six feet and two inches tall. He has wide shoulders and forearms and healthy and vast muscle mass with a stocky build and is fair in complexion. He has beautiful curly black hair and dimples that show a smiling facial expression, and he is very handsome with dark brown eyes. Bert always wanted to feel very important and insisted that I treat him that way; admiration should have been his first name. He wanted to be always admired and reminded me that he was very important and didn't care about anyone's feelings but his own. Bert made no excuses for his demands and feelings that he was entitled to, and his needs were always more important than mine or anyone else.

Bert graduated from high school. He was very good at using his hands, so he joined a company as an apprentice and obtained a construction trade. He pursued his passion and graduated with vocational education in trade and industry. Bert is a hard worker and mastered his construction trade, especially building foundations using concrete materials.

Bert's Characteristics

Bert enjoyed boxing and pursued his passion as a light heavyweight boxer and enjoyed it when he fought his opponents and beat them until they were bloody. Bert was very social and spent many days a week hanging out with his friends and talking about current events and women's jobs and responsibilities. He felt strongly that a woman's place is in the kitchen, and her sole responsibility is to take care of her husband and his needs and their children along with cooking and cleaning, and this was his favorite saying. Bert loves action movies at Strand Cinema movie house. His favorite action movie was Enter the Dragon starring Bruce Lee. He loves and owns Rolex watches, expensive designer sweaters, and Clark's men's shoes. His favorite color was brown. His favorite foods were chicken, including curried, fried, and stew served with white rice, steamed cabbage, and salad, including sliced cucumber. He loved Cadbury chocolate with nuts and hot popcorn from Demico House.

Always about Bert's Needs

Bert wanted us to be married when I turned 16 years, but I never agreed to this verbal contract with him. He became restless and angry because I disagreed with his want for us to get married. I began to feel pressure and panic; therefore, I began to use delaying tactics as my 16th birthday came and went because he made me feel very uncomfortable. He became angry because he had previously asked permission from my great-grandmother, my guardian. My guardian told him my parents would have to consent to the marriage, but he did not want to hear that. He was not happy; however, he continued to present himself as attentive, kind, and very loving until he couldn't get his way. He would try to buy my love by giving me his entire paycheck, which I always refused. He did not want me to have any friends or relationships, not even with family members. He became highly possessive and jealous and forbade me to be in relationships with peers, including family and friends. I felt that my world was closing in – therefore, at the first opportunity for a vacation that was presented to me by my maternal aunt, Olivia, I packed a suitcase and was ready to sail on a four-day trip to Matthews Ridge, my destination in the Northwest Region, as I previously stated.

Way of Escape

I accepted my aunt's invitation for this vacation. Before my departure on vacation, Bert showed up at my home to forbid me to leave on vacation. He grabbed my suitcase, and we got into a physical confrontation with, me trying to recover my suitcase, which he refused to return to me. He disappeared with it. I grabbed a small shopping bag, threw a few pieces of clothing in it, ran to and caught the city bus to the Lady North Court ferry, boarded it, hid in the cabin, and refused to come out until the ferry sailed. Before the ferry sailing, I saw Bert with my suitcase as I peeked out the cabin window. He also boarded the ferry. He came to the cabin window and pleaded with me to get off and return home with him. I refused, and he finally had to get off because the ferry was preparing to set sail.

Two weeks later, Bert showed up with my suitcase at the front door of my grandmother's home in Matthews Ridge. I was surprised about how he found me and my grandmother's home. My grandmother welcomed him, and he was now also staying in the same home. He wanted to continue the marriage agreement; however, I reminded him that I left to get away from him, and that did not change. Bert was a charmer, and my grandmother simply liked him.

He refused to stay away from me, and he was even more persistent so that I began to feel smothered and suffocated, which caused me to verbally state that the marriage plans were terminated because he became possessive, jealous, and demanding whenever he saw me with anyone, period. He began to verbally threaten me frequently, and I ignored him but was very cautious around him. I began to feel intimidated when alone with him, and I would try to get out of the home and not be left alone. He became violent and began inappropriate and crazy behavior when he saw me speaking to especially males. On one occasion, at a party, as I spoke to a male whom I had become friends with, he came toward me and demanded that I leave with him; I refused, and he threatened me again.

Early the next day, he approached me to inquire if I was going to the picnic the next day. He requested me not to go, and if I did, he said he would physically hurt me when I returned. He further said that if he couldn't marry me, then no one else would. I ignored him, but this day before the picnic, I was left alone in the house with him. I was not fortunate because he wrestled me to the floor and raped me in my grandmother's home. He told me I better not say anything to anyone, or he would hurt me badly. I was so shaken up and traumatized and angry to know that he wanted to marry me but thought nothing of raping her. I left that house as fast as I could and went to my other cousin's home. I did not return until I was sure somebody else was home.

I was afraid of Bert and afraid to tell anyone about this rape. I was certainly not going to tell my grandmother, Maria, because years ago, when I told her about the rape and sexual molestation, she slapped me because, as my grandmother put it, "… a godly man Young was lied upon." The next day, I was at the picnic with my family, and Bert was there. And he approached me and demanded I leave with him; he then proceeded to pull me, and I began to struggle -- he eventually let me go because my friends and my families would not have tolerated him abusing me. He therefore left, and later that day, I got on a truck with my oldest cousin and rode back to the village from the picnic, and I was dropped off at the Community Center.

The Holy Spirit whispered to me to run and just don't stop. I took off at lightning speed. I ran long-distance track in those days, and I could run. As I was running, the Holy Spirit told me to look back, and when I did, I saw Bert chasing me. Therefore, I continued to run even faster. As I drew near Maria's home, Bert continued to chase me. He couldn't catch me because I was a very fast runner. I did not stop running until I ran up the stairs of Maria's home and into her house. Bert then caught me in the house and beat me severely; my face, arms, legs, and different parts of my body were bloody, swollen, and bruised; this took place while my older uncles and cousin observed and laughed.

Even though I forgave Bert, I refused to maintain any relationship with him. He left Maria's house to return to the city, but not before he apologized and tried to get me to return to Georgetown, in the city with him. I never even looked at him and only nodded at his apology. I did not utter a single word to him.

About a week after this act of violence, I was playing a game called sword fence with one of my oldest cousins, Tony, who observed when Bert physically assaulted me, and he laughed. Tony and I both had a knife as pretend swords. And as we spar playing the game with the knife, I got tired and did not want to play any longer, so I raised my right hand in surrender and simultaneously yelled stop; it was too late when I yelled stop because his knife came down on my wrist and he stabbed me with his knife. His knife got stuck into the bone of my right wrist, and two people had to struggle to pull this knife out of my bone. There was blood gushing all over.

Tony, my cousin, and I ran to the hospital about two miles away for emergency medical assistance. As I was running, I began to black out -- I began to lose consciousness and had to be carried to the hospital by Tony. Looking back, I now realize that the summer of 1975 appeared to be the worst one of my life, but it was a blessing in disguise. I know that despite these different trials and tribulations in my life, God did not allow these things or people to end my life because God loves me so much. God will use these tribulations to bless others who cannot use their testimonies to set the captives free.

Courage to be Different

I understand that whatsoever you allow in your life, God also will allow, simply because He has no authority on earth because God has leased earth to man. God is so faithful that He will not break His own Word. I also understand that God wants us to permit Him to get involved in our lives and for us to make Him Lord in and over our lives. According to King James Version, "And God said, Let us make man in our image, after our likeness: and let them have dominion over the fish of the sea, and over the fowl of the air, and over the cattle, and over all the earth, and over every creeping thing that creepeth upon the earth (Genesis 1:26).

I know that God loves me so much that He has given me stewardship and dominion of the earth, legal authority over it, and everything on it.

What are your reflections on the questions below?

Have you ever experienced jealousy in any of your relationship? _____

_____

_____

_____

_____

How did you handle insecurities in your partner's behavior? _____

_____

_____

_____

_____

What was this jealousy like? _____

_____

_____

_____

_____

How is conflict in marriage handled in your family? _____

_____

_____

_____

_____

Have you ever experienced being stuck? _____

_____

_____

_____

_____

How would you handle being stuck? _____

_____

_____

_____

_____

How would you deal with an overly jealous partner? _____

_____

_____

_____

_____

How would you interact with a partner that shows his/her insecurities?

_____

_____

_____

_____

What do you do when you don't feel heard in your relationship? _____

_____

_____

_____

_____

Have you ever experienced domestic violence in a relationship? _____

_____

_____

_____

_____

How do you feel when your partner is not emotionally present? _____

_____

_____

_____

_____

How did you feel after you were threatened? _____

_____

_____

_____

_____

What do you do when your partner is not emotionally available for you? _____

_____

_____

_____

_____

Are you married? _____

_____

_____

_____

At what age were you married? _____

_____

_____

_____

How did you meet your spouse? _____

_____

_____

_____

Were you ever forced to do anything that you did not want to do?

_____

_____

_____

_____

How did you handle being bully? _____

_____

_____

_____

Do you know of anyone that was rape? _____

_____

_____

_____

What advice do you have for someone that was rape? _____

_____

_____

_____

_____

Have you ever been rape? _____

_____

_____

_____

_____

Has anyone ever made you feel unsafe? _____

_____

_____

_____

_____

Do you know of anyone that had a physical confrontation with his or her abuser? _____

_____

_____

_____

_____

Do you know the Scripture Genesis 1:26? What does this mean to you?

_____

_____

_____

_____

_____

Reconnect To The Vine And Yearning to Belong

My mother, the Giver, gave birth to my two last male siblings for her partner, Ralph; now, my mother has seven children. We continued to live in Matthews Ridge in the Northwest Region of Guyana, South America. A shift occurred in my family when my mother shared with us that she was moving to the United States with my third and fourth siblings because my brother's godparents were sponsoring them to relocate to the United States.

Foundation Shift Again

I was unsure how to take this news, especially since I felt abandoned by Giver and John during my early childhood. Now again, Giver was leaving and this time to go far away, and I had no idea what my life would be like. I had gotten used to living in the country with my siblings and another family close, and now I was told that Leila, my great grandmother, Giver's grandmother would be our caretaker and Ralph, Giver's partner. Things happened very quickly, and the next thing I knew, we were all traveling to Georgetown in preparation for Giver and my siblings to relocate to the United States. They did leave for the United States, and the rest of us returned to Matthews Ridge to live with my caregivers, Ralph and Leila. These were very confusing times for me because I now had to get used to another caretaker's personality, Leila, along with Ralph, that was not my father.

Near Miss

On one occasion, I became very ill; my entire body was swollen due to an allergic reaction from breathing in sea turtle meat as Ralph was cooking it to entertain his friends. I had to be physically carried by Ralph, my care giver to the hospital. I was unable to walk and began to have breathing problems. At the hospital, I received injections to stop my entire body's swelling and enable me to breathe.

Within the next year, I was told we were all moving back to live in Georgetown, Guyana, in Agricola Village because Ralph was leaving to join Giver in the United States. We packed up, left Matthews Ridge for good, and relocated to Georgetown, Guyana, in Agricola Village. Ralph left and went to the United States, and he and Giver married and lived with my two siblings.

Becoming the Care Giver

At about ten years old, I was responsible for caring for my three younger brothers and doing household chores. I ensured my brothers were clean, so I bathed them daily, creamed their bodies, fed them, did their homework daily, and maintained proper bedtime. I washed and ironed their clothing and ensured they were always presentable at home and in the community. I took such pride in caring for my brothers, and it came to be such pleasure when they were clean, looked good, adequately fed, attended school, and did well in school and the community.

Struggling in School

I attended elementary school as I struggled to academically perform at the proper grade level. During this period, teachers were allowed to use bamboo canes, belts, or rulers to beat me because my academic performance was not at grade level. I received many beatings because I was slow at processing information. I could not function or manage my study, and my habits were poor compared to my peers in the same grade. I had many difficulties processing information accurately, let alone passing examinations. I was barely making it in school. My peers enjoyed teasing me and calling me names, and they bullied me. I was so shy and withdrawn that I would often be afraid to sit in my seat in the class for fear of being called by the teachers and not knowing the right answer, which would lead to a beating by the teachers and teasing by my classmates. The teachers would often beat me and make me stand on the chair in class so that the entire grade could see me. I never really fit in my circle of classmates. I was somewhat accepted by peers whose parents were poor or those who felt sorry for my plight. Many times,

I was unable to maintain or comprehend the schoolwork. I was easily distracted and would infrequently remember to write assignments down. Time management was a challenge because, by the time I got my three brothers ready for school, I was late, and it was automatic that by the time I ran to school, the Headmistress would be waiting at the door.

My school had two doors only, and after the late bell rang, the front door would be shut, and the only entrance was at the back door. After prayers were said in the morning or after lunch, the Headmistress would be at the back door with a cane in hand to deliver lashes that landed on any part of my body. I spent much time in class in escape mode by easily daydreaming because it made me feel safe, and I would come back to reality with a cane lash on my back from the teacher.

Giver remembers me

My only faith and hope were a correspondence from my mother, Giver, which sometimes accompanied money. My mother would send a barrel with clothes and other supplies for my four siblings and me, sometimes twice a year. At times, pictures would follow. These were precious moments for me when I received a letter addressed to me from my mother, Giver. I felt so special and honored to receive a mail addressing me and all about me.

Neglected by Maria

Some of my most painful experiences were from Maria, my grandmother, living in Guyana in Matthews Ridge. She wrote to my aunt, Olivia, which lived on the second floor above where I live, and she sent money and foodstuff to Olivia and her children, and at no time would she even write or send my siblings and me anything – not even during the holidays or for our birthdays. Maria would send sacks of foodstuffs for my cousins and Olivia, and they would never share with us. Even when Maria visited, she would not give me not even a candy – she would say, "Your mother is in the United States of America."

Education is a Weapon

I was still struggling to read, write, and understand my academic work. I became tired of being tired, so I began sounding words out to teach me how to read, speak well, and understand how to write. I decided that if I was ever going to learn how to read and write, I would have to do it on my own, and that is just what I did. I did not trust the teachers since their focus was to use canes to beat but not to teach.

I stayed close by when my older sister read; I asked my sister to read out loud, and I began to imitate my sister's pronunciation of words, and I would repeat them. My sister continued to read aloud, and I had her use her fingers as she read the words. I looked at the words and listened to them, and then I began practicing and imitating my sister. According to the Bible in King James, Now unto him that is able to do exceeding abundantly above all that we ask or think, according to the power that worketh in us, (Ephesians 3:20). I began to read for hours, repeated this pattern, and just forced myself to read aloud. I spent every minute reading, rereading, reading, writing, and repeating. This lasted for many months until I began to read a book a month, then every three weeks, to every two weeks to every week. I increased my speed in reading until I was reading about five books a week in the afternoon and past midnight after school, chores, homework, and caring for my three youngest brothers.

Effective Co-Parenting

I made sure that my brothers did their homework and took their showers, and were fed. I nurtured them and watched them ensure they were safe and not hurt. I enjoyed caring for my siblings. During that time, I was responsible for fetching water daily from the pipe at the street corner. On the weekends, I got on my knees, scrubbed and polished floors, and did laundry from about 6:00 am until completed. Twice a month, I was responsible for ironing a barrel of clothes; most of the day on Saturday and part of Sunday after church.

Escaping to Peaceful Places

I enjoyed these chores because they allowed my mind to daydream about places that were so beautiful and peaceful -- and as I continued to daydream, I would plan things and complete them as I mentally thought about them. I enjoyed making pocketbooks, floral arrangements of flowers, crocheting different garments, and creating and designing leather sandals in my spare time.

Reflect and Answer the Questions Below

Have you ever lived apart from your biological family? _____

_____

_____

_____

_____

Who did you live with? _____

_____

_____

_____

_____

Who discipline you? _____

_____

_____

_____

_____

How were you discipline? _____

_____

_____

_____

_____

Have you felt disconnection from your biological family? _____

_____

_____

_____

_____

What did you do? _____

_____

_____

_____

_____

How old were you? _____

_____

_____

_____

_____

Do you know of others that were raised without parents? _____

_____

_____

_____

_____

Have you ever been rejected by your family? _____

_____

_____

_____

_____

How does rejection by your family feels to you? _____

_____

_____

_____

_____

What is your relationship now with your family? _____

_____

_____

_____

_____

Do you think that a person can feel disconnected while living with their family? _____

_____

_____

_____

_____

What does disconnection look like? _____

_____

_____

_____

_____

What advice do you have for parents that have not bonded with their children? _____

_____

_____

_____

_____

What do you think is most important, material things or nurture? __

_____

_____

_____

_____

Do you think that nurturing someone has an expiration time? _____

_____

_____

_____

_____

Why do you feel that nurturing is important? _____

_____

_____

_____

_____

Who are you connected to in your family? _____

_____

_____

_____

_____

Do you have a relationship with God? _____

_____

_____

_____

_____

How would you describe your relationship with God? _____

_____

_____

_____

_____

Do you think that is important to be connected to God? _____

_____

_____

_____

_____

Have you experienced feelings of wanting to be validating by family and friends? _____

_____

_____

_____

_____

What would happen if you never received validation? _____

_____

_____

_____

_____

What is your relationship like with your children? _____

_____

_____

_____

_____

Do you think that it is important for you to connect to your children and loved ones? _____

_____

_____

_____

_____

What is one way that a parent can connect to his child? _____

_____

_____

_____

_____

The Dream Came Through At Its Appointed Time

One day I looked up, and before me was a woman coming out of a taxicab with overseas luggage. This woman looked familiar but was relatively thin. Could this be Giver, my mother finally returning? This couldn't be possible because no one said anything in the house where Giver was visiting Guyana, South America. Wow, it was my mother who finally returned, alone.

Feelings of Rejection by Giver

I ran through our front door barefoot with excitement, speechless to hug my mother with my arms extended towards her. But Giver never extended her arms towards me. One look at her face, her expression was of annoyance and displeasure. Indeed, my mother would be happy to see me at last. The Giver was different, though. She was not at all so glad to see me. I wonder what could I have done wrong that made her that upset? Is Giver embarrassed to see me? Is it my face? My clothes? My body? Instead, Giver yelled at me, saying I needed to put shoes on before greeting her; wow! Giver never greeted me but instead ordered me to get back into the house.

During Giver's visit, whenever I would leave the house walking in the yard or on the street barefoot, Giver got upset and had no problem yelling at me and saying how embarrassed she was with my appearance. The way I dressed in my clothes upset her; not wearing my shoes upset her. Giver's reactions and comments confused me because I felt she had a cultural conflict. Leila, my great-grandmother, forbids me to wear good shoes unless I was going to church or some place of importance, which was on rare occasions, and now Giver, my mother, forbade me to be barefoot outdoors, period. I was so happy during Giver, my mother's visit – when my mother went out, I would run excitedly to greet her. I would sit and wait on the steps with my eyes fixed on every car that passed by to see if the car was going to stop in front of my house and if Giver had returned from her errands. But Giver, my mother, would be so embarrassed to greet me if she saw me on the street, especially if I forgot to put on footwear, which I was not accustomed to. For many years, I did not wear footwear to school – only when I got into the older grades was I allowed.

Differences in Cultures

During Giver's first visit back to Guyana, I was confused because I was clueless as to what to do to please Giver. I understood two things: to not go to greet Giver, my mother, and never to be caught without footwear outside the house. After Giver returned to the United States of America, her first set of letters was about how embarrassed she was with my appearance, my form of greetings, and me walking barefoot on the street. My mother also wrote a letter saying that their friends found me walking on the street barefoot when I went to greet them. These friends sponsored my mother and siblings in the United States.

The things that people make as a conversation to get me into trouble were incredible. I now realized that the years that Giver was physically out of my life and the longing to see her again and when I did see her brought me peace but discontent because of her reaction to what she felt was important. I felt that Giver never emotionally connected with me, and it was all about my presentation and clothing but never about my emotions, feelings, or thoughts. According to the Bible in the (KJV) 1 Samuel 16:7, But the Lord said unto Samuel, Look not on his countenance, or on the height of his stature; because I have refused him: for the Lord seeth not as man seeth; for man looketh on the outward appearance, but the Lord looketh on the heart.

Coming Face to Face With my Siblings

Giver, my mother, returned to Guyana, South America, for the second time. This time she was accompanied by my third and fourth siblings to receive their permanent alien registration cards for immigration purposes. I was happy to see them after so many years with us living apart in South America and North America. This time

I was very cautious when Giver appeared with her children, for I did not run to greet them when they showed up from the airport. I waited patiently for them to walk through the gate toward the front door. I greeted them with words, but I did not extend my hand to embrace them, nor did they extend their hand to embrace me.

If I didn't know that they were my family, I would think that they were strangers that showed up or me meeting them for the first time. They came with no excitement and barely greeted us, and I became guarded instantly. After a while, I tried to engage my siblings and spend time with them, but there was no emotional contact, so I remained cordial during their visit. Reflecting on my siblings' behavior when they left years ago compared to their behavior when they came back as teenagers, I was very disappointed with them. At that moment, I swore that I would never be like them. They were different, though. The first couple of days, they appeared excited. Still, something about them was strange, and this made me feel uneasy, especially since this time, my other four siblings and I were now coming to live as a family with our parents and these two siblings in the United States. From that moment, I became very uneasy and wondered what life would be like with a family that presents as strangers and detached. Since then, I often wonder if living in the United States causes people to forget their foundations, cultures, roots, relationships, and communications and to lose the significance of family.

Did Your Life Turn Out the Way, You Planned It?

Have you experienced your life not turning out the way you plan? __

_____

_____

_____

_____

What was different in your life? _____

_____

_____

_____

How did this make you feel? _____

_____

_____

_____

_____

What adjustments did you make, if any? _____

_____

_____

_____

_____

Were you disappointed? _____

_____

_____

_____

Did you share these feelings with the persons involved? _____

_____

_____

_____

Did you pray to God and seek Him for answered? _____

_____

_____

_____

What was that feeling like to know that God has answered your prayer?

_____

_____

_____

_____

Were you pleased when God answered your prayer? _____

_____

_____

_____

_____

Did you thank God for answering your prayer? _____
_____
_____
_____
_____

Did you have any foresight that what you have prayed for would have turned out that way? _____
_____
_____
_____
_____

What did you do when you realized that things did not turn out as planned? _____
_____
_____
_____
_____

How do you handle disappointments? _____
_____
_____
_____
_____

How do you deal with regret? _____
_____
_____
_____
_____

How did you handle disappointment from parents? _____
_____
_____
_____
_____

What is faith? _____
_____
_____

_____

_____

How does faith come? _____

_____

_____

_____

_____

What pleases God? _____

_____

_____

_____

_____

Do you blame yourself for decisions you've made that did not turn out as you planned? _____

_____

_____

_____

_____

Did you blame people for disappointing you? _____

_____

_____

_____

_____

Did you blame God? _____

_____

_____

_____

_____

Were you able to pick the broken pieces of your plans up? _____

_____

_____

_____

What did you do with those broken pieces? _____

_____

_____

_____

_____

Did you confront the people that disappointed you? _____

_____

_____

_____

_____

Are you still in a relationship with these people? _____

_____

_____

_____

_____

What is that relationship like? _____

_____

_____

_____

_____

Transition into a New Beginning of the Unknown

Quotation: *When God sends us, He has specific purpose and plans by Gurmay Effrige Fraser*

My four siblings and I relocated to the United States in Brooklyn, New York, when my mother returned to Guyana and got us when I was sixteen years old. I was reunited with my third and fourth siblings and Ralph, Giver's husband. I was so happy to see my sister and brother, but that wore thin fast when my sister and brother began to show their dislike for me.

My brother, my sister, and I all attended the same high school; my brother and I were in the eleventh grade, and my brother and I were in the same first-period class. One disadvantage I found with being in the same grade and class as my brother was that I felt that whenever he was late for his first-period class, our teacher always inquired of me about his attendance, and sometimes this became bothersome because the entire class of students would turn their gaze to me to hear what I had to say. During those times, I was very shy and did not like speaking, especially when I was asked to respond.

The Enemies Within

My sister also attended the same high school. I soon learned that this was not a good idea because she frequently cut classes, she reported that she never liked school, and her actions showed it. This sister was very often upset with me when I refused to join her. She and her friends cut class and left the school building. Eventually, this sister dropped out of school, and she stayed upset with me because I stayed in school and graduated from high school.

There were always fights and arguments at home among the siblings, especially since we all shared a tiny apartment at that time; a one-bedroom apartment. This sister and brother made me feel like a stranger, and I did not belong there. They complained that they had to share their things, watching television was problematic, and my brother would turn the television to a show he wanted whenever he came home and found me watching television. These siblings' behaviors reminded me of bullies. They spent time thinking up ways and doing things that were so painful, whether it was eating all my dinner or using up the supplies of my goods, and they told me that I was not welcome in the house, and they suggested that I should return to Guyana, South America where I was born. To be at peace and to have my own money, I signed up for a special program in my high school called cooperative education, and this afforded me to work one week and attend high school the following week. I began to learn job skills, get my own money, and meet a different quality of working people in the many job assignments I held.

The Mercies of God

I began to feel isolated and lonely and spent many nights crying. My mother worked in a different borough away from home as a live-in housekeeper for rich white people and would generally come home only once a month or once every six weeks. This sister took a special interest in abusing me. She frequently stole my money and, on one occasion, forged my signature and withdrew my money from my savings account in the bank. On other occasions, she stole my clothes and shoes and would give these to her friends, whatever items would not fit her. My other clothing, she would cut them up or rip them into threads. Looking back, I realized that her spirit was always wicked.

I avoided the tribulations with her by engaging in continuing education classes and extracurricular activities while I was in high school. At times, upon my return home, she would have eaten up all dinner and, on most nights, would tease me to start a physical confrontation. I always had a small, well-proportion body structure; she was taller than me and overweight. So, she used her overweight body to intimidate me and rush up to me to knock me out of the way.

111

Even when I was not in her way, she would act as though she did not see me and push me out of the way.

How Much More Should I Suffer

I would ignore her by reading, watching television, or doing extra homework for extra credit. She would switch the channel on the television or turn the lights off while I was reading, or she would begin speaking by using profanity. Only my Abba Father has kept me in perfect peace on all occasions. During these times, I placed all my energy into graduating from high school. I struggled to pass my classes because my brain, due to the poison at 3-month-old, was still causing me challenges in many of my learning.

I spent much time rereading and trying to comprehend my schoolwork. I was eventually able to graduate from South Shore High School. I began to become intentional about my life and future, and I planned for my future and prepared to leave Giver and Ralph's home so as not to end up in a place I chose not to mention.

Wickedness and Sibling Jealousy

Then to compound matters, I began dating Brey, this guy who appeared to be nice; I was able to tell him my problems and confide in him. When I met him, I was not interested in any relationship or friendship. I only needed someone to share my feelings with, and unfortunately, it did not turn out that way. I began to date him before long, and I believe due to isolation, rejection, loneliness, and abandonment a shift occurred. Being in a new country and living in a home with siblings with toxic behaviors, I began to find comfort in Brey because he appeared to listen to me and show me attention, or so I thought. After many months the conversation with Brey turned into a relationship, and I became distracted in this relationship. I did not qualify him before spiritually and physically becoming involved with him.

I also then found out that I was pregnant, and then he was not at all nice, and my sister also found out about the pregnancy, and she became so vicious that I became afraid that she was not mentally stable, nor did I feel emotionally or physically safe around her. Therefore I did not trust her judgment. Her emotional instability and dangerous behaviors showed up when she would place pins and needles in my bed. The pins and needles would stick all over my skin when I lay in bed, and she would laugh hilarious. This continued right through to the seventh month of my pregnancy.

Planning my Escape Route

Simultaneously, I attended Kingsborough Community college full time at night while working a full-time job during the day, up to two weeks before my baby's birth. I quickly began to plan a future for myself and my unborn baby. I juggled traveling on the trains and buses on public transportation, leaving home before 7:00 in the morning and returning around midnight after school. This continued right up to my ninth month of pregnancy when the professors requested that I should not return until after my baby was born.

Before my daughter's birth, I lay in bed in severe pain while my baby was in the breech position with complications, struggling to be born. The continuous pain got my attention, and my mother, the Giver, accompanied me to the hospital. The doctors sent me back home on two different occasions that night, but the pain got more intense, and I returned to the hospital within hours because I felt something was wrong with my unborn baby. Upon examination, the doctors realized the complications of the breech position of my daughter too late, and they could not perform a cesarean section. The doctor had to manually turn my baby into a birthing position for my baby to be delivered alive. My baby was over eight pounds at birth. When I contacted Brey, my baby's father, while I was being rushed to the hospital, Brey's whereabouts were unknown. He couldn't be found anywhere. Days later, he showed up with many reasons why he was not physically or emotionally available, but these were merely excuses.

Wicked Nanny

I returned to college when my baby was one week old, and I left my baby in the care of a babysitter living in the same apartment building I was living in with my family. I was attending college, and while in my abnormal psychology class, I had a vision of my baby crying, and it was as though I was hearing her crying with this shrilling sound. I saw her in that vision, and she had been crying for a while because her eyes were puffy and swollen. At that moment, my professor looked at me, called my name, and asked me if everything was fine. I answered in a shaky voice, "no," and said I must go home to my baby. He said I could leave the class, and I ran out of the class as quickly as I could. I ran down the stairs to the first pay phone available to call the babysitter. I did call the babysitter just to hear my baby screaming in the background. I sprinted to the bus stop, and an hour later, I was at the babysitter's front door. I pushed past the babysitter, grabbed my baby, and ran to the hospital around the corner.

At the hospital, my baby was seen immediately because she was still screaming. My baby was injured while in this babysitter's care because the babysitter pulled my daughter's left ulna out of joint; this caused severe swelling, and after that incident, I switched to attending college in the daytime and took my baby to college in public transportation and arranged my peers in taking turns to watch my baby while I was in class. Money was not available for childcare, and I refused to be a burden on the government with welfare. I was not going to compromise my baby's future by not being able to provide for her. Brey gave whenever he felt like it, which was mostly next to nothing, and he was not responsible as a parent, and I decided not to become distracted by his shortcomings. I knew that weeping might endure for a night, but God said joy cometh in the morning. I also knew there was a time and a season for everything, including my pursuit of obtaining my Associate of Arts Degree.

Praise God in the Unknown for the Breakthrough

Do you know the plans of God for your life? _____

_____

_____

_____

_____

Have you ever doubted the plans of God for you? _____

_____

_____

_____

_____

Do you know God's purpose for your life? _____

_____

_____

_____

_____

Have you ever been separated from your loved ones? _____

_____

_____

_____

_____

How long were you separated from them? _____

_____

_____

_____

_____

Why were you separated from them? _____

_____

_____

_____

_____

Have you forgiven your family for abusing you? _____

_____

_____

_____

_____

Did your family accept you? Yes/No _____

_____

_____

_____

What was that like to know that you were accepted by your family?

_____

_____

_____

_____

_____

How did this make you feel that your family did not accept you? ____

_____

_____

_____

_____

How did you engage with family knowing that you were not accepted by them? _____

_____

_____

_____

_____

When was the first time you felt rejected by family member/s? _____

_____

_____

_____

_____

Was it important for you to be validated by these family members? ___

_____

_____

_____

_____

Did you forgive your family for abusing you? _____

_____

_____

_____

_____

How were you abuse? _____

_____

_____

_____

How long did this abuse last? _____

_____

_____

_____

_____

Who abuse you? _____

_____

_____

_____

_____

What were the red flags of the abuse you sustained? _____

_____

_____

_____

_____

Were you able to be protected by your parents/adults from the abuser?

_____

_____

_____

_____

_____

Have you experienced abuse from your parents/sibling/s? _____

_____

_____

_____

_____

What did you do? _____

_____

_____

_____

_____

Did you get help? _____

_____

_____

_____

_____

Were you abuse while pregnant? _____

_____

_____

_____

_____

What was the abuse like? _____

_____

_____

_____

_____

Was this abuse by a loved one? _____

_____

_____

_____

_____

How did this make you feel? _____

_____

_____

_____

_____

Did you have children prior to marriage? _____

_____

_____

_____

_____

How did you manage to raise them? _____

_____

_____

_____

_____

Did you work during pregnancy? _____

_____

_____

_____

_____

Did you have any difficulties with your pregnancy? _____

_____

_____

_____

_____

Did you or your baby have difficulties with the delivery? _____

_____

_____

_____

_____

Did you get help from your family after your baby was born? _____

_____

_____

_____

_____

Were you able to return to work/school? _____

_____

_____

_____

_____

Did you work while attending school/college? _____

_____

_____

_____

_____

Did you work while raising your children? _____

_____

_____

_____

_____

Did you attend school/college and work simultaneously while raising your children? _____

_____

_____

_____

_____

How did you manage to balance work and raising a family as a single parent? _____

_____

_____

_____

What resources or network was available to you? _____

_____

_____

_____

Did you receive any support from the children's father or/and family?

_____

_____

_____

Did you receive government subsidy to help you raise your child/children? _____

_____

_____

_____

How long did you receive government subsidy? _____

_____

_____

_____

What subsidy did you receive? _____

_____

_____

_____

_____

What structure/boundaries did you implement at home? _____

_____

_____

_____

_____

What about routines for your family? _____

_____

_____

_____

_____

How did you implement accountability with your family? _____

_____

_____

_____

_____

Were you involved in parent-teacher meetings? _____

_____

_____

_____

_____

Did you graduate from school/college? _____

_____

_____

_____

_____

Are you working in the field of your degree? _____

_____

_____

_____

_____

Are you emotionally available with your family? _____

_____

_____

_____

_____

Are you emotionally present with your family? _____

_____

_____

_____

_____

Single Parenting with Intimacy

Quotation: *Assignments are given for a specific time and season, and with specific task that leads to destiny by Gurmay Effrige Fraser*

I continued to attend college as I struggled academically, financially, and with new responsibilities as a teenage single parent. During this season, up until my daughter was two years old, I lived with my mother, Giver, and her husband Ralph, my stepfather, and five of my siblings in a 2-bedroom apartment on the first floor in Brooklyn, New York.

Covenant Relationships is Vital

My day began at 5:00 am Monday through Friday until midnight. I took three buses to travel to drop my infant daughter to the babysitter. Then take three buses in another direction to work at 8:15 am. After work ended at 3:15 pm, I sprinted to get on two different buses to college for 4:15 pm and then walked under a mile to my building on the college campus. When I finally returned home from full-time work and full-time college, a quick dinner at that hour and quick preparation for my baby and myself to start the next day all over again. Thank God for my mother, Giver. She has been a great support for me. Picking up my daughter from the babysitter after she left work, bathing and feeding my baby, and putting her to bed for me. This new babysitter was a sure blessing to my baby and me.

Infidel Father

You would think that my daughter's father, Brey, would be ashamed that he was physically and emotionally unavailable during my pregnancy, our daughter's birthing process, and her birth. He continued to lack commitment by not providing finances or assisting with parenting. Even in our relationship and fatherhood, he continued to make excuses about his physical and emotional absences. When I approached Brey about his behavior, he made several excuses and remained inconsistent and unavailable most times. According to the KJV Bible 1 Timothy 5:8, it reads *But if any provide not for his own, and especially for those of his own house, he hath denied the faith, and is worse than an infidel.* Brey continued to have his adulterous relationships, and his whereabouts were sometimes unknown.

Giver, my mother, and I continued coordinating my daughter's childcare pick up and drop off Monday through Friday. I continued to juggle work and school full time. I continued to struggle academically, with many C grades. My college expelled me from school and placed me on academic suspension due to poor academic performance, and during that time, I was not allowed to attend college.

I then enrolled in an airline travel school in New York City after work Monday through Thursday evening, and I did very well. Upon graduation, I was offered an airline job traveling to many countries and being gone for days and sometimes weeks, but I refused to take that job that would cause me to be away from my baby. I desire to reapply to college because I know that education and the application of knowledge are critical for my life. I was not going to allow expulsion from this college or any other to prevent me from achieving my education and making a stable life for myself and my children. Receiving public assistance and being subject to social service was not my consideration. After six months, I reapplied to Kingsborough Community College and got accepted. I worked hard enough to raise my grades, and my grade point average was elevated above a C, just high enough to be eligible to graduate. I finally graduated from Kingsborough Community College with my Associate of Arts Degree with a C grade point average. I did it with the help of God. I don't compare myself to anyone but myself.

Affliction from Jealous Family

My schedule was more complex, and it consisted of taking my baby to the babysitter and a different location now, rushing to work, and after work running to get my bus at a specific time to get to classes on time. Simultaneously, my sister continued to emotionally and physically abuse me, and she would alternate from eating most of my dinner or enjoy spitting in my food unbeknownst to me. It was not until a long time after when she would boast to other family members about how she spits in my dinner, and I would come home and eat it. Other times, she would steal my money when I cashed my paycheck at the check cashing and have all my cash in my pocketbook because I couldn't get to the bank to deposit it. She continued to destroy my clothing, books, college work, and any of my belongings she chose or purposely used up all my baby supplies, milk, cereal, pampers, and lotion for her son. When I approached her, she would become violent and threatening and use her body; she was big and heavy and charged toward me, and I had to move out of the way to prevent her from knocking me down.

Living at home became so unbearable that I ran from home, and at age twenty-one, I found an apartment for my baby and myself where I felt safe because I did not trust my mother's youngest daughter around me or my baby. I was afraid that she would put something in my food and my baby's food and milk to cause us to be ill since she had no problem spitting in my food and using up my baby's food.

In the Bible, many stories are provided of families: it was King David's son that raped his sister; Cain killed Abel; some of Joseph's brothers plotted to kill him but sold him into slavery.

You are who God says you are

I did not leave Brey, my daughter's father, right away; he always had an excuse for why he couldn't be responsible. Maybe I thought that I could change him. I was constantly feeling sorry for him and his issues and denying myself the peace and joy I could give myself if he wasn't in my life. One day he told me that his brother had died; however, he would not allow me to visit his home to show my respect for his dead. I later was told that he had a girlfriend staying there while she was on vacation from one of the United States service agencies. This woman accompanied him to Guyana, South America, to bury his dead. I did not share this information with him, but I called him while he was in Guyana, and this woman answered his hotel telephone. When I spoke to him, he was shocked that he was caught in his lie. He returned to New York with more lies.

You must be the Change You Seek

I stayed with Brey in his infidelity and the domestic violence he inflicted on me because I wanted my daughter to have her father since my biological father was not in my life. Brey was always missing in action, and he was always physically and emotionally absent and unavailable. However, Brey announced some months after that, that he was on his way to Guyana because his mother had orchestrated his marriage to his dead brother's wife. I then told him that was fine, but this time the relationship would end when he got on the plane. The next day, I called the airline and confirmed that he was on the plane. I then went to the hardware store to purchase new door locks, and I changed my locks. When he returned to the United States, he came to my apartment while I was at college. He was allowed into the apartment by Maria, my grandmother, who spent time with me and my daughter at my apartment.

When I came home that night from college, I immediately knew something was wrong because I did not hear my daughter's voice, nor did she come to greet me as I opened my apartment door. I panicked when I found out that Brey returned from his trip. He came to my apartment and took our daughter. I was so angry when I found this out that I nearly lost it. I called him on the phone and demanded he brings our daughter home immediately. He shortly rang the doorbell, and when I opened my apartment door, he had my daughter hidden behind him. He punched me in my face and screamed that he knew that I was cheating on him. He then gave me our daughter. I dumped Brey instantly after he busted my face with blood gushing over the floor. My relationship with Brey was officially ended that moment.

You Get What You Tolerate

A few years later, I dated and fell in love with my second child's father, Mr. Unavailable, and this relationship resulted in me getting pregnant by my Mr. Unavailable. Mr. Unavailable is eight years older than me, and, in my mind, I thought that because Unavailable is older, he would be attentive, emotionally available, emotionally present, kind, loving, faithful, purpose-driven, and possibly marriage material. But I quickly realized that what we had going on was always about Mr. Unavailable. It was about his career, his music, his sisters' whims, his relaxation and maybe if he feels better then he'll decide if we can see each other. Mr. Unavailable clearly stated that I should never just show up at his basement apartment unannounced because this is not tolerated. Unavailable even gave me a scenario: if he ever dropped his wallet in my apartment, would I go through his wallet, and of course, I said, "No."

Our baby was born at 11 lbs. 3 oz, a natural full-term gestation delivery, and a handsome little boy with lots of complications in delivery. But God! Thank God my son was delivered without any complications with him or me. Mr. Unavailable began to show some interest in our son's care, like putting our son to bed, holding him, and feeding him, and took us grocery shopping three times, period; and he visited more while our son was an infant. Mr. Unavailable then went back to his normal engagement twice a week, Thursday and Sunday nights, unless in the Summer when we will go to a park once. Mr. Unavailable was very self-centered and self-fish and cared only about his needs. Mr. Unavailable was very cheap and meagerly contributed to our son's childcare twice a month until our son was four years old, which was the end of any financial support. When a man doesn't provide for his home, he is worse than an infidel.

New Season of Change

I continued to attend college and work full-time simultaneously. One day one of my co-workers invited me to her sister's grandson's birthday party. I did attend with my children, my daughter, and my unborn baby. The location was beautiful and peaceful, and the home was brand new. The community was beautiful, and water surrounded this community, and it felt energized and full of life. I fell in love with that community, and the next workday, I began to inquire my friend about the builder and how I could find out more about buying a house. The community was new, and many homes were projected to be built there. To this day, my friend made all kinds of excuses about how busy her sister was and couldn't get the information from her.

Faith Pleases God

Fortunately, by pure accident, I found out that another co-worker lived in that community and bought the home that she is living in. I began pestering my co-worker for the information about the housing, and for over a month, this new co-worker kept dodging me and making all excuses that she did not know or have the information. I was persistent, and I told her that I would continue to annoy her until she got that information for me. Reluctantly, after this co-worker realized that I was not giving up, one day, she threw a piece of paper at me and said that I had two numbers; call them and see what you find out but please don't bother me any further. I thanked her and called both numbers, and finally, a workman answered and provided me with the number to the realtor.

I called the realtor and introduced myself, shared why I was calling, and asked her to provide me with the address of her location. She said that there are no 3-bedroom homes available or being built now. She told me to keep in touch, and I told her I was coming after work today. She urged me not to come, and I insisted that I was coming and that I only needed to see the location.

Faith that is not tested cannot be Trusted

When I arrived at her office, she said, "you should not have come," and you are pregnant. She then asked me how I got there, and I told her that I walked and then took a train and a bus. She invited me into the office, then showed me the plans for the current homes and the future homes to be built. I was as engrossed as I looked at the graphs and imagined what life would be like for my children and me living in the community in our own home.

Shortly after, I heard someone coming through the door, and as I turned my gaze, I saw the postman giving her white envelopes. I then returned my gaze and began to imagine living in a brand-new house with my children. I heard her opening the envelopes, and she said, "wow," the bank rejected three of the proposed homeowners' applications, and now there are three homes available. The realtor told me you now have three homes available for you. Which one would you like? I said you work in this neighborhood and are familiar with this community. If you were to buy any of these three homes, which one would you buy? She said I would buy the end corner house and then explained the features and benefits to me. I turned to her and said then that's the one I am purchasing.

She gave me the entire application package, and I filled it out and returned the package to her, and placed it in her hand. I have never seen my home, not on the inside or in the surrounding areas. I closed on my first home on December 21, 1985. Before I close on my home, I could describe every area because God has shown me the inside of my home many times. I was in my home, even in my dream, before I physically walked into my home. At closing, my daughter, aged seven years, and my son, aged three months old, were present, and after we closed on our home and got to our home, it was exactly as I had seen my home in my dreams. I smelled the newness of the carpets and saw the beautiful colors of the cabinets and the décor of the bathroom and the other rooms, and our home was beautiful.

I was 26 years old, the youngest homeowner in the community, and my beautiful babies and I moved into our home.

I knew no one in that community but thanked God for His grace: He blessed me with a good babysitter who was able to care for my two children. I also vow to myself that I will protect my children and not allow them to be abused in any way. I refused to marry either of my children's fathers because I realized they were not responsible, and I would not have my kids suffer or have additional problems in their lives. I felt that the abuses I had sustained in my life were enough for the three of us.

One day I had enough of Mr. Unavailable and ended that relationship and informed him that I would not take him to court for child support if he didn't feel that it was his responsibility to provide for his son, then let that responsibility rest upon his conscience.

Training up my Children in the Ways of God

I remember spending hours daily tutoring my children and preparing them for the State examinations. Initially, my daughter enjoyed the tutoring time with me, while her brother rejected the time. My daughter began to resist being tutored, and after I explored with my daughter about her lack of interest, my daughter told me that her teacher told her she would never make it into the gifted and talented middle school. So, my daughter said it was useless for me to tutor her; I rejected what her teacher told her and continued to encourage her. I told her not to say anything to her teacher because her teacher does

129

not know the gifts that God placed in her. I spend enough time with my daughter cultivating and stirring up those gifts that my daughter has, and when she took the NY state examinations, she scored in the top 1% nationwide every year. Then my daughter took the entrance examination for the middle school for the gifted and talented, she scored in the top 1% in academics and special talent in art, and she was qualified for the gifted and talented program in the middle school in our neighborhood.

I had an opportunity to meet my daughter's teacher again at graduation; the teacher reminded my daughter of the school that she had chosen for my daughter. This school was unsafe in the slums with high drug traffic, gangs, crime, and project buildings. I answered the teacher and told her that her negative comment was an inspiration and that my daughter was accepted into the gifted and talented middle school instead; the same one that the teacher felt that my daughter was not good enough to attend.

Intimacy with my Children

I spent quality time with my children, listened to hard conversations that were sometimes painful, encouraged and supported them when I knew that they would excel, and at times was firm when I could see no benefit but a trap of the defeated devil to derail my children. I was not always a great parent, but being a parent to my two blessed children had imparted great patience and revelation knowledge about what to do and not to do as I struggled the many years as a single parent when their fathers and their fathers' family looked on to see how I would mess up. I enjoyed nurturing my children, providing for their needs and care, and empowering them to be the best that God said they could be. I disciplined them in love.

My Seeds are Mighty on Earth

My children attended college with me while I was in classes at Kingsborough, Medgar Evers, Adelphi, and Fordham, so they know what struggles and sacrifices felt and look like. They understand what accomplishments and graduations look and feel like. While I was in class, my children were doing their homework. My children were never suspended nor held over; they graduated from elementary, middle, high school, and colleges. Even though both of my children's fathers never financially supported them nor cared for their children, I did not become distracted by their fathers' lack of involvement. That did not stop me from loving and caring for my children without taking either child's father to court for child support. I believe that one day both of my children's fathers will have to answer to God. The God that I serve is a God of generation. God will judge us parents as good parents based on the legacy that we establish for ourselves and our children, our grandchildren, and our great-grandchildren.

Parent Train Your Children up in Ways that they should go

How did you raise your child/children? _____
_____
_____
_____
_____

Who helped you with raising your children? _____
_____
_____
_____
_____

Did you ever have to run away from situations to ensure your child or children were safe? _____
_____
_____
_____
_____

What does parenting means to you? _____
_____
_____
_____
_____

What are/were your parenting styles? _____
_____
_____

_____

_____

What techniques have you used to parent your child/ children? _____

_____

_____

_____

_____

Did your husband's parenting style different from yours? _____

_____

_____

_____

_____

How were you parent as a child? _____

_____

_____

_____

_____

Is your parenting style different from how you were parent? _____

_____

_____

_____

_____

Have you stayed in an abusive relationship? Why? _____

_____

_____

_____

_____

Have you remained in an abusive relationship because of your children?

_____

_____

_____

_____

In today's times, what is your suggestion to parents who have dealt with, or may be dealing with some of the same traumatic events when

raising their kids? _____
_____
_____
_____
_____

Now you are the Parent, and Your Life is the Mirror

How would you rate the relationship with your child/children's father?
_____
_____
_____
_____
_____

Have you ever been in a blended family? _____
_____
_____
_____

What was that like for you in a blended family as a parent? _____
_____
_____
_____

Was your husband or child father ever married? _____
_____
_____
_____

Did your husband or child father have other children? _____
_____
_____
_____

What was his relationship with these children? _____
_____
_____

_____

_____

How was his relationship with the mother of the child/children? ____

_____

_____

_____

Did/do you have a relationship with that child/children's mother? __

_____

_____

_____

Do you allow your children to socialize with their father's children? __

_____

_____

_____

Why? Why not? _____

_____

_____

_____

How does your child/children feel about his sibling/s? _____

_____

_____

_____

Is your child/children's father involved in your child's life? _____

_____

_____

_____

Is the father involved in your child's education? _____

_____

_____

_____

_____

Did your child/children spend time with his/her father? _____

_____

_____

_____

_____

How is the child monitored or supervised? _____

_____

_____

_____

_____

What is your child's behavior like when she/he returns from visiting their father? _____

_____

_____

_____

_____

Has your child ever been taken by a parent without informing you? __

_____

_____

_____

_____

How did that make you feel? _____

_____

_____

_____

_____

Did you think that he was going to return your child? _____

_____

_____

_____

_____

Who helped you raise your child/children? _____

_____

_____

_____

_____

Did you use a babysitter or daycare for co-parenting your child/ren? __

_____

_____

_____

How would you rate the babysitter or daycare experience? _____

_____

_____

_____

Did you feel that your child/children were safe? _____

_____

_____

_____

Did any of the child/ren ever got hurt at the daycare or babysitter? __

_____

_____

_____

What was your relationship with your childcare provider? _____

_____

_____

_____

What advise do you have for single parents? _____

_____

_____

_____

Have your children ever been abused? _____

_____

_____
_____
_____

How do you ensure that your children are safe? _____

_____
_____
_____

Do you sit with your children and review homework assignment? ___

_____
_____
_____

Do you assign household chores to your children? _____

_____
_____
_____

How are you involved with your children's school? _____

_____
_____
_____

How do you nurture your child/children's potentials? _____

_____
_____
_____

How are you a Role model to your children? _____

_____
_____
_____

Have you ever taken your child/children's father to court for child support? _____

_____

_____

_____

_____

Are you training up your child/children in the ways that they should go?

_____

_____

_____

_____

_____

New Births of Rewards and Blessings in Parenting

I was able to work full time during the day and attend full-time evening college; I attended other colleges, not sure of what I wanted to do. I tried several different careers; however, I became so bored with some of the classes that I also changed many colleges as I continued to search for my niche. I continued to be dissatisfied with many of the education programs and switched from college to college for one reason. Giver, my mother suspected my struggle and encouraged me to attend an orientation at Adelphi University off-campus on Varick Street in New York City. This school started a bachelor's program called ANSWER for prospective students.

My biggest challenge was my poor academic grades, a C average from Kingsborough Community College, and continuing my pursuit of higher education. My challenges were how I was going to be able to improve my academic performance at a university when I was unable to get grades above a B in a community college. I felt that I was not smart enough and that a university was for academically bright students on the honor roll and those who received honors. I decided to apply anyway at Adelphi University, and I was hoping that I would be rejected to save myself the embarrassment of being accepted and then kicked out of school for poor academic performance.

God would have it that I got accepted at Adelphi University on a provisional basis with stipulations that I had to receive all A's and one B only in my first semester. Another challenge I faced was coordinating my responsibilities as a single parent; my after-school and childcare responsibilities, working full time with emotionally disturbed middle school students, attending and completing my internship, and everything that comes with managing time, money, and family. Money was very tight for me, and I had the sole responsibility of caring for both of my young children independently of their fathers. That refused the responsibilities of co-parenting and providing any finance for anything. I had no personal transportation and had to travel simultaneously on public transportation from full-time work to full-time school and internship. I reluctantly accepted this college placement, even though I wanted to reject it. I claimed I had enough of my problems that I didn't know how to solve, and I had no interest in listening to anyone's problems. I continued to work full-time during the day.

My babysitter began to show inconsistency in her service of caring for my children, and I did not feel that I could trust her caring for my children. Therefore, from work, I picked my children up from their school and took them with me three nights a week to classes at Adelphi University. While I was in my classes, my children sat in the college lounge and completed their schoolwork while having snacks and playing board games.

I began to develop study habits and schedule how I planned to complete my weekly studies. I did well, and I was able to remain in the ANSWER program. I graduated with my bachelor's degree with a three-point grade point average in two years. It was hard work, given all my responsibilities, but it has taught me how to be responsible and accountable as a mother and as a person. Then the day of my graduation came from Adelphi University, held at the main campus in Long Island, New York. I was anxious and worried about getting there on time. Mr. Unavailable was accompanying and driving us to the graduation. He came early in the morning from a party and needed to sleep longer than he should, and he did have a hard time getting up on time. When Mr. Unavailable finally got up late, he was rushing, and we barely made it on time before my graduation commencement.

At my graduation, when my name was called to get my diploma at Adelphi University, my 4-year-old son stood up on his chair and yelled, "yes, that's my mommy." I was so encouraged and inspired by his comment that it motivated me to apply to graduate school. I then applied at Fordham University and was accepted into the master's degree program and attended full time on Saturday from 9:00 AM to 6:00 PM; while teaching special education in the New York City school system full time and attending field placement Monday through Thursday after work towards my master's degree requirement. I slept about an hour each night during the week while I was attending this program. This master's degree was an advanced program, and I graduated with my master's degree within one year, magna cum laude. Both of my children attended Fordham University on Saturdays while I attended Fordham University.

During a part of this journey, I was able to get another babysitter from the neighborhood to provide childcare from Mondays through Fridays. However, problems arose when the babysitter came to live with my children and me. The babysitter did not like my oldest child and would delegate her paid responsibilities to my daughter. I came home one day and heard the babysitter coming down the stairs from the second floor to the first floor, and the sitter did not know I was home. The sitter was banging a scissor on the stairs and speaking very loudly, saying that she would take the scissor and stab my daughter with it. My daughter was running down the stairs in front of the sitter with a terrified look on her face, and the sitter was chasing behind my daughter. Behind the sitter was my baby, crawling down the stairs. I stepped in front of my daughter when she got to the bottom of the stairs and grabbed my daughter out of the babysitter's way. The sitter was shocked when she stepped in front of me and became speechless. I told the sitter that she would never touch my daughter or my son and remain in our home. I ordered the sitter to pack and get out now, or else. I then fired the sitter and refused to bring anyone else into our home around my innocent children.

The episode with the babysitter empowered me and increased my desire to continue my education and spend more time with my children because I couldn't trust anyone to take care of my children even when I paid for this service. Dropping out of college was not an option, and stopping was not an option, and I still couldn't depend on either of my children's fathers. When life comes at you hard, you must go after life hard and with force and precision, and just focus on the possibilities – nothing else.

141

Your Reflections, Views and your experiences in Parenting

Is it a challenge to coordinate your responsibilities as a parent (single/married)? _____

_____

_____

_____

_____

What are your thoughts about managing your money, time and family?

_____

_____

_____

_____

_____

How did you manage childcare, work issues and relationship? _____

_____

_____

_____

_____

Was your relationship affected by your responsibilities of family and work? _____

_____

_____

_____

_____

Did you attend college, work full time while raising your children? __

_____

_____

_____

_____

How did you set structures and routines in your home? _____

_____

_____

_____

_____

What are some of the things that you have tried as a parent that was successful? _____

_____

_____

_____

_____

What things that you have tried that were unsuccessful? _____

_____

_____

_____

_____

Did you have any problems with childcare service for your children?

_____

_____

_____

_____

_____

Were your child/ren babysat? _____

_____

_____

_____

_____

Did you have more than two (2) babysitters for any of your children? Why? _____

_____

_____

_____

_____

Did you go to a babysitter? How long were you babysat? _____

_____

_____

_____

_____

Did you like your babysitter? Why? Why not? _____

_____

_____

_____

_____

Searching For What's Missing

Quotation: *Until we activate the gifts that are hidden in us, we will continue to search on the outside for what's missing by Gurmay Effrige Fraser*

God created Adam only; everything Adam needed came from what God placed in him, including all generations. I remember attending church three times a week, which was mandatory. However, these church folks were kind of strange. The women wore very long clothing with their heads tied up, and it was called a turban, a headpiece. While in church, both men and women did a lot of hollering, especially when they would announce that the world was coming to an end. Well, this confused me, and then I was unsure why someone would continue to attend church when all that was preached was the world was coming to an end. Many of these church folks, when I met them on the street -- oh, they were so mean, and as a matter of fact, some of them were my elementary school teachers. I believed they abused their authority, especially when it came to beating with that cane made of bamboo. I was very silent and figured that if I stayed quiet, they would think that I was indeed stupid and leave me alone.

Society and our families tell us to go to college, get a good education, get a good job, get married, buy a house, and work until retirement to get good benefits, a good pension, and health insurance. I became frustrated with myself -- I went to and graduated from several colleges, bought houses, had several jobs, and got married. I realized that I was more frustrated because I fell out of alignment with my passion and things became so crazy in my life. I just couldn't put my finger on why things were not aligned in my life since I did what society recommended. It appeared that the harder I worked, the worse things became. During those times, I was working at three different jobs simultaneously. For as long as I can remember, I have always felt a void or emptiness in my spirit. There were many times that I couldn't explain these feelings.

Therefore, I spent many years of my life saturating myself with many activities, such as acquiring knowledge in arts and crafts, sewing, first aid, nursing, business, teaching, culinary arts, Girl Scouts, Brownies, home nursing, and multilevel marketing including Amway, Mary Kay, Avon, real estate, life insurance, etc. I tried many professional careers and obtained education and licensure in these areas: teaching special education, social work (clinical and administrative), school social work, businesses: marketing and entrepreneurship, and many other business courses.

I began college with a focus on psychiatry; then, I switched to accounting, occupational therapy, and computer science and was still unfulfilled and empty. I worked in several professions: a group home, assistant teacher, therapist, administrator, trainer, auditor, supervisor, social worker, daycare, senior health care, early intervention official designee, track star, landlord, seamstress, culinary art, designing my clothes, etc. Still bored and searching, I then developed a thirst for reading and read extensively, a minimum of about five books weekly. As a matter of fact, in my spare time, I spent more time reading than eating or sleeping, or hanging out.

During the period 1988-1993, I worked full time, attended college full time, was involved in clinical hours for my social work BS and MSW; I was working a part-time job, I was a single parent with two young children, and I was managing my own private home and my multilevel apartment building, providing property management service, for over ten years to my real estates. I bought my first property at the age of 26 years old. During these years, I was not driving. I graduated with my BS in two years- 9/1988 -- 5/20/1990; and continued to graduate from university, and I got my MSW in one-year 9/1990 -- 9/1991. I took both degrees with honors while teaching full-time and working part-time jobs. My children never missed school unless they were ill, which was rare; they also scored in the 90-98th percentile on state examinations nationwide because I tutored both kids daily.

My children's fathers were very much alive but were never involved in the care of their children. I believe, according to the children's fathers, that their activities were always more important than spending time assisting in raising their children or providing financial support.

I continued to search for that missing link and thing, but I did not find anything. I developed a thirst for knowledge but was unsure as to what was causing that void in my life. Until I found God and studied to show myself approved by His Word for my life, I stopped looking at the outside, the environment. I then began looking at the inside of my heart and life experiences, and then I started to run like the wind. I then began to manage my time better because I realized that I needed to become the best version of myself, do the things that I'm passionate about, and help the people God has assigned me to help.

I repented and changed my mind as I began to meditate on the Word of God for my life. I got up, I arose, and the glory of the Lord is shining in and over my life. Now it's time for you to get up from whatever situation, health issues, circumstances, relationships, financial hardships, or/and whatever you're facing. Begin to speak positive words over your life. Our Word frames our world. Stop saying what you don't have, complaining, talking negative words about your life, or agreeing with others' words that are negative that they speak over your life. Start saying what God says that you can have, who God says that you are. Our words frame our world, allowing others to speak negative words or words that don't align with God's Word over our lives is unacceptable. Nothing grieves God more than the disbelief and doubt that we speak and allow others to speak, or what we tacitly agree to when we are silent when others are speaking things that God has not said in His Word for our lives.

Remember, life and death are in the power of our tongue, our words – speak life only. Arise and shine and understand that we are seated in Heavenly places in Christ Jesus. All the negative things that have happened to us or are happening to us are outside forces. Arise, Greater is He (the Holy Spirit) in us than he (principalities) in the world. Arise, Arise, Arise. Keep saying it until you believe it; I did. Remember that God is no respecter of man, child, person, or thing, idea, or situation; God is the only respecter of His Word. When we study, use, and apply His principles in His Word, they will work for us. God is a legal God, and He watches over His Word for our lives to perform His Word. His Word is a law onto Him, and His words shall not return to Him void. His Word is what we must meditate on day and night so that when the enemy tries to distract us or place people in our lives to speak against the Word of God, we can boldly declare the Word of God for our goals, situation, and event. I am convinced that I deserve the best that God has for me, and I continue to go after it by putting God first and by using His Word to destroy generational curses, iniquities, transgressions, regions of captivity and strongholds from my life, my children, our family, and everyone that God has placed in my life. Wait, the best is here now.

How do you take care of your spiritual, physical, mental, relational, financial well-being?

Do you know your purpose? _____
_____
_____
_____
_____

How can you find your purpose? _____
_____
_____
_____
_____

What problem were you called to serve? _____
_____
_____
_____
_____

What situation, issues or things upsets you? _____
_____
_____
_____
_____

What are your spiritual gifts? _____
_____
_____
_____
_____

The Holy Spirit gave gifts to men and women; do you know what your spiritual gifts are? _____
_____
_____
_____
_____

Do you know if what you are doing is your vocation? _____
_____
_____
_____
_____

If it is not, what are you going to do about it? _____
_____
_____
_____
_____

Do you attend a church building? _____
_____
_____
_____
_____

What does "you are the church" means to you? _____
_____
_____
_____
_____

Have you ever searched for something but not find it? _____
_____
_____
_____
_____

Have you found yourself? _____
_____
_____
_____
_____

Have you found Abba Father? _____
_____
_____
_____
_____

Who are you? _____
_____
_____
_____
_____

Do you have a daily relationship with God? _____
_____
_____
_____
_____

How do you know when you find what's missing? _____
_____
_____
_____
_____

Whose are you? _____
_____
_____
_____
_____

Now that you know your purpose, when will you get serious to activate it? _____
_____
_____
_____
_____

How do you share your gifts with the world? _____

_____

_____

_____

_____

Trials, Tributations, But Still Standing

Quotation: *When we don't believe in ourselves, we permit unauthorized people to misuse us by Gurmay Effrige Fraser*

My daughter's father's Brey's family never liked me-- they thought that I thought I was better than they were. I overheard Brey's father telling Brey that I would be an educated woman, and with my light complexion, I would have no use for him because he is dark skin. The truth was I would have no use for Brey eventually because Brey was very physically and emotionally abusive. Besides Brey being a lousy boyfriend, he was a terrible father that misunderstood his responsibilities as a father and was not responsible for caring for our daughter, not financially or emotionally.

At age 21, I graduated with an Associate of Arts Degree and moved myself and my baby into my first apartment. Brey continued with his adulterous relationships and, in addition, began to physically abuse me. On one occasion, I almost lost my left eye because Brey hit me in the face over my left eye with a wine bottle at his birthday celebration that I hosted in my apartment. He claimed that I was flirting with his sister's husband, and his sister and her husband were the only two guests he had invited to our small celebration. His sister's husband was looking through my picture album and saw a picture of me that was taken at a studio when I was considering modeling. My hair had a beautiful light brown color, and my hair was flowing down my back; and his brother-in-law asked me who was this beautiful young woman, and I tapped him on his elbow and said it was me. His brother-in-law turned and looked at me and asked me if we had a chaser for his liquor, and I turned to Brey and asked him what a chaser was. Brey then grabbed the liquor bottle and struck me across the left side of my face, began to curse me, calling me all kinds of names, and then accused me of flirting in front of him with his brother-in-law. Oh, Brey was so jealous and always accused me of having affairs while his continued. I always knew that this family didn't like me, and I was used to hearing people's negative projections, especially since I had heard this all my life and in some of my own families. I was used to being rejected and ignored.

On Thanksgiving Day 1982, Brey persuaded me to accompany him to his family for Thanksgiving dinner, I did not want to, and I shared this thought with him. He insisted that he wanted me to come and that his family had nothing against me. I did not believe him, but eventually, I accepted and went with him along with my baby girl. During dinner, the woman Brey was having an affair with showed up, and they got into a physical confrontation in my presence. Shortly after she left, Brey and I got into a physical confrontation because he wanted me to talk about the affair that he was having, and I refused. Brey's mother came on the scene and told them that every time I showed up, I was always a problem, and over her dead body would Brey marry me. Funny, I was crying because Brey had pulled my right thumb so hard that he nearly dislocated it to get me to talk about his affair with this woman. I, however, was empowered when his mother stated that over her dead body would her son marry me. I wiped my tears instantly and stopped crying, and I reported to Brey's mother that Brey was not marriage material, and instead, I would never marry him, and I didn't.

I was afflicted many times with sicknesses, trials, and tribulations. I recalled slipping on some floor polish at work at United Cerebral Palsy in Brooklyn, New York, tearing ligaments in my left knee and pain, and returning to work for fear of losing my job. Another incident occurred while I was at work in Brooklyn, New York as a Teacher's Assistant in Special Education with emotionally disturbed middle school students. I accompanied my class on a trip when gangs in New York City attacked my class. Many of the students were teasing these gang members by calling them names and making weird gestures, and I saw that these gang members began following us, and they were coming to attack my students and my class. I began to run and instructed my students to run, and when we got to our location, I stood at the building door and pushed all my students to safety. Then the gang members pushed me into the wall, and I was thrown to the other side of the wall; I hit the right side of my head with such force that I was thrown towards the building door, which was metal and glass, where I hit the left side of my face before I was thrown to the floor with a bang. I appeared to have fallen asleep, and when I woke up, I was on the floor; all the adults stepped over me and left me there on the floor, and I was trampled. I suffered from a concussion and severe headaches that lasted many years.

While I was a special education teacher in New York City, one of my students pushed his classroom chair into my right knee. My knee was immediately swollen to the size of a small watermelon, and the ligaments were damaged. My knee was sprain and misaligned. I had severe pain day and night and lots of problems transitioning from one position to another and falling. I was required to walk with a protective device to balance my body because many times, my knees would buckle, and I would fall.

To make matters worse in my home, my bedrooms and full bath were on the second floor of my home, and it was a trying experience to walk to the second floor for many months. I was seen by the Department of Education medical doctors, who saw nothing wrong and discharged me back to work. I never returned because they based their decision without ordering any examination or extras or MRI. During that time, I needed months of physical therapy and required surgery after suffering for two years before surgery. During the surgery, I was counseled by the Anesthesiologist, but he forgot to tell me that I would receive a needle in my lower spine with the spinal tap. When the other Anesthesiologist inserted the needle into my lower back during the surgery, I jumped. This long needle was bent and formed a circle when the doctor and nurse pulled it out of my spine. They both let out a scream and said that I was not supposed to move, let alone jump. After the surgery, I had to wear a leg brace and receive physical therapy for many weeks.

Years later, I met an older man who manipulated me into moving into my home by saying he had a problem with his ex. At that time, he was living in the basement apartment of their shared home, and he feared that he would do something bad and end up in jail. He called me crying and saying he had no place to go, and he kept crying, and as much as I was helping him to process his other options, he rejected them with one excuse after another. Reluctantly I allowed him to move into my home with the condition that he could only be here for three months. This sounded good during those moments, but I never held him accountable, and he ended up living in my home for two years. During that time, he and I got engaged.

After a while, I wrote a business plan and a policy and procedure manual, and we started a business; shortly afterward, I found out that he was cheating on me and was engaged in an adulterous relationship. He began to slack up on the business responsibility that he had agreed to in our business. This man began to threaten me that he would leave because he felt unappreciated. One day he decided to move and left with my vehicle while emptying the business bank account and stealing our business debit card. Our business was supposed to be housed in my home in the extension I built.

This same man called me the next day and wanted to report to work; instead, I fired him. I then contacted a moving company and packed his stuff, and in three days had his belongings moved into storage with the bill paid up for one month. I then allowed this company to release his belongings to the Salvation Army if he did not pay the storage bill beyond the month that I paid for. I went to the post office and removed his name from my address; I then closed the business account. Afterward, I closed and restarted the business structure; had his car removed from my property; changed my locks, mailbox keys, and the code to my house alarm.

A few years later, I met my then-husband Conroy, who promised me the world. Before the marriage, we both received marriage counseling. I was specific and stated the things I would not tolerate in our marriage: abuse, adultery, dishonesty, and lack of communication. Conroy swore to love and cherish me for as long as we both shall live. Our wedding vows were broken in less than a year; he was having an affair, and I could feel that he was drifting and emotionally distancing even when we were in conversation. One day, as I was about to take my truck for service, the Holy Spirit said to me to look in the glove compartment, and I quickly followed the Holy Spirit's instruction, and

155

there I found a condom. When I questioned Conroy about this, he denied the intent of the condom by justifying why it was in my truck.

During this time, I developed a cough without a cold. I also began to feel a pain in my left rib cage and suffered from lots of sweat at night, which caused me to change my clothes at least three times during the night. Conroy convinced me to visit the doctor, and my son drove me to my private doctor, who diagnosed me with low hemoglobin levels and inflammation in my left rib cage. My cough became severe with excessive perspiration, and within three days, Conroy took me to the emergency room at the neighborhood hospital, Coney Island, where I was admitted.

During hospitalization, I was diagnosed in June 2005 with a rare Pheochromocytoma, a 4 cm tumor that grew out of my left adrenaline gland above my kidney. This tumor was positioned on my spine when I was first diagnosed. I met with the medical team, who provided me with options to properly diagnose the tumor. I was told that many risks were involved with all the options needed to determine the tumor. I was highly allergic to one of the major chemical elements required in the procedure.

Before my medical diagnosis, I was involved in intercessory prayer every morning at 5:00 AM, and now I went into fasting and praying in addition to worshiping and praising God. I also began extensive research about my medical diagnosis. I returned to the hospital with the medical team in place, and the guarded CT scan was done to assess the tumor. Doctors placed two extra-long needles in my back, closed to my spine, to extract fluid from the tumor. This caused the tumor to double in size in less than two weeks. Emergency surgery was warranted because my heart rate and blood pressure levels were dangerously high, and the medications were ineffective. I had surgery that I was told would take about three hours, but my recovery into consciousness took over fourteen hours due to medical complications during surgery. Conroy was working for my company, and I was now forced to return to work because they would be no money coming into the house for expenses. I returned to work four days after this major surgery, unknown to my doctors, children, and family.

Simultaneously, I discovered that Conroy pretended that he had ended his adulterous relationship with his previous lover. However, I began doing some research and then confronted him because I found out this was not so. When confronted, of course, he became abusive and pulled my hair; he held it for a good five minutes. As I further discussed his inappropriate behaviors and deception, he angrily hit me with a severe blow across my chest. This caused me not to breathe at that moment but thank You, my Abba Father, that you have revived me and safe me with Your Breath. I was told that because I was a born-again Christian, I needed to try counseling and not give up on my marriage. Therefore, Conroy and I met for counseling with the pastor who married us.

I refinanced my home in New York and reluctantly gave in to Conroy's request to explore buying a home in Georgia, so a house was found, and he went down to Georgia to sign the contract. Conroy was supposed to bring the contract for me to sign, but he came up with excuses, and I never signed the contract. We discussed the upcoming closing of the Georgia home. I requested Conroy to have the attorney mail the closing documents to me. He became very angry and told me that he had a problem and that I did not trust him. I told him that he did not trust me. Because of my work as an Independent Contractor, only Conroy was present at the closing of our home. He did not include my name on the closing document, including the deed.

Another betrayal occurred when Conroy had an affair with a woman he met online, and even though he denied the affair to the pastor during our counseling session, he did admit it to me. He promised to be a better and more faithful husband. Conroy, I, and my son moved from New York to Georgia because Conroy stated that he felt the family would be able to make a better life there. I gave up my job, sold my home in New York, and started again from the beginning because I was told that I must listen to my husband because he is the head of the household. Within two months, he was involved in another adulterous affair, and this unfolded while I accompanied him on the road as he was making his deliveries for his job. He was a truck driver. When confronted, he became enraged and yanked and pulled my hair from the roots. I had to struggle to get free, and soon after, I called

911 but could not be helped because we were driving through West Virginia on his 18-wheeler truck with a trailer.

This made him furious, and he began to use profanity and threatened me. He then proceeded to push me out of the eighteen-wheeler truck as he was driving at a speed of over 70 miles an hour. The first opportunity I got, I jumped out, penniless, and ran. I sat on the side of the road and cried for a while as I tried to figure out what I would do. I was traumatized and felt so betrayed as I processed that he was trying to kill me. I couldn't believe that this was happening.

I continued in this abusive marriage with much discontentment. I called the woman Conroy was having an affair with, confronted her, and spoke with her seven times. The last time I spoke with this woman, I told her that I would never contact her again, and if she chose to continue to see my then husband, that was between them and God, for I had already spoken to God about it and His decision is all that matters to me.

Some time afterward, when I tried to speak to Conroy about the physical and verbal abuse and attempted murder, he stated that I made him angry because I accused him of untrue things. He blamed me and told me that I did not want him to have friends and was always accusing him of infidelity. During the same time, I shared with Conroy the information that this woman told me about their affair. Conroy became angry and told me that this woman was stupid to report to me the details of their affair and that this woman was not good because usually, most women he knows would never speak to the wife, let alone discuss the affair. When I asked Conroy about the onset of his affair and its duration, he was surprised that I knew so much. I also reported to Conroy that shortly after we met for counseling that Conroy requested from our pastor, Conroy had started this affair while I was still in New York working. When he was confronted with this information, he accused me of not being a good wife and not being supportive of him.

On the same day, April.10.2006, when Conroy left for work, God spoke to me and told me to get out of the house. I did not leave that day. I had a severe headache when Conroy pulled my hair while on the road trip. Later that day, God told me to take a shower, and while I was in the shower, God told me to place my hand on the left side of my neck. I was shocked at what was there. A very large lump, and when I touched it, the headache got worst. I then began to pray, and while I was still touching the lump, it shrunk, and the headache disappeared simultaneously.

The next day around the same time the previous day that God told me to leave, God spoke again, and this time God said that I must leave by April 13.2006. God did not have to speak to me again about this. I told God that I had no money to leave, and God directed me about where to get money and how much to take for the trip. Within hours, I packed some things, got the money for gas and food, and drove to Atlanta to stay at a friend's house; I was going to rent her basement apartment. My son and I spent overnight at this friend's house. That was not God's plan. I got up the next morning and went to the closet to get some clothes as I planned to travel to Charlotte, North Carolina, on my way to New York. God spoke sternly to me, "God said, I made you the head, and now you have made yourself the tail." God said, "You will not live in anyone's basement apartment." I was scared because I knew I was disobedient to God's plan for my life. I quickly repented and now had to process how I would get my belongings out of this basement. Shortly after, I left and drove to Charlotte, North Carolina. Less than twenty-four hours the owner of the house called me to report that I couldn't rent her basement. I told her that I already knew because I was already told so.

I prayed and asked God where He wanted me to live. God responded that I was going to get my answer in church. I attended church in Charlotte that Sunday with both of my children. As I was praising and worshiping in church, the pastor delivered a very powerful message, and just as the message was done, I told God that I still did not know where God wanted me to live. God said for me to me still. I continued to pray and worship, and then the church elder did an alter call for members who needed prayer for a job. I again asked God where He wanted me to live. God's swift response was I must be still. I continued to pray and worship God, and there appeared stillness in the church. I again spoke to God and asked where He wanted me to live, and this time God said, "Be still and know that I am God." Right after, the elder made an altar call for anyone who wanted to know where God had assigned them to live to come forth. I can't explain this, but I felt that I was moving from the pew as I was lifted off the ground as I moved toward the front of the church. Now I was standing in front of the elder, the only one answering the altar call.

As I stood there, God answered me, and He whispered into my right ear, God said, "North Carolina it is." I then relocated to North Carolina; and found an apartment for my son and myself. I had to start my life all over, laying my foundation and learning about life in the south. One great blessing was that God had sent my daughter to North Carolina to live, so the transition was not too painful. Conroy did not stop pursuing me and wanting us to get back together. Eventually, I gave in and permitted Conroy and allowed him to move into my apartment, and he did join me to live in North Carolina about four months later.

Conroy then claimed that he was now a born-again Christian and was sorry for the abuses. Conroy began to pressure me to return to Georgia. For a moment, I thought about it but then declined his offer. I refused to go back when God told me to get out. Conroy then reported that if I didn't return to Georgia, he would be forced to get a woman and return to Georgia and live in the home that I bought with my money. I told him that he was free to do what pleased him.

But my son and I were staying in North Carolina because God did not tell me to return to Georgia. Conroy asked me why I took him back, and my response was that God told me to leave the house in Georgia God did not say at that time to leave him.

What are your reflects on the questions below:

Rejection

Have you ever been rejected? _____
_____
_____
_____
_____

Is rejection good or bad? _____
_____
_____

_____

_____

What does rejection feel like? _____

_____

_____

_____

_____

How did you handle the rejection? _____

_____

_____

_____

_____

Did you feel that you needed to change things about you or possible things around you? _____

_____

_____

_____

_____

What did you do about the rejection? _____

_____

_____

_____

_____

How did you feel being rejected? _____

_____

_____

_____

_____

Is there a difference between rejection and betrayal? _____

_____

_____

_____

_____

How do you move on from being rejected? _____

_____

_____
_____
_____

How do you feel about the person/s that rejected you? _____
_____
_____
_____
_____

Was this person a family member? _____
_____
_____
_____
_____

What lessons have you learned from the rejection? _____
_____
_____
_____
_____

How do you describe your life prior to being rejected? _____
_____
_____
_____
_____

How is your life after the rejection? _____
_____
_____
_____
_____

How do you handle relationships since the rejection? _____
_____
_____
_____
_____

Would you allow yourself to experience rejection again? _____
_____

_____

_____

_____

Can you stop anyone from rejecting you? _____

_____

_____

_____

_____

How do you prevent being rejected again? _____

_____

_____

_____

_____

Have you discussed rejection with your children? _____

_____

_____

_____

_____

Did you discuss previous rejection with your spouse? _____

_____

_____

_____

_____

Obedience:

How do you remain obedient to God? _____

_____

_____

_____

_____

What does God say in His Word about obedience? _____

_____

_____

_____

_____

What does obedience mean? _____

_____

_____

_____

_____

How do you demonstrate obedience? _____

_____

_____

_____

_____

Do you feel that you need to be obedient to your boss? _____

_____

_____

_____

_____

Are you obedient to your job? _____

_____

_____

_____

_____

Do you demonstrate obedience on your job? _____

_____

_____

_____

_____

How do you practice obedience in your family? _____

_____

_____

_____

_____

Do you educate your children about being obedient? _____

_____

_____

_____

_____

How do you hold your children accountable to being obedient? ____

_____

_____

_____

_____

How do you communicate obedience? _____

_____

_____

_____

_____

Does obedience and listening belong in the same sentence? _____

_____

_____

_____

_____

Do you consider yourself to be a good listener? _____

_____

_____

_____

_____

What do you think is involved in listening? _____

_____

_____

_____

_____

What are you listening for? _____

_____

_____

_____

_____

Why are you listening? _____

_____

_____

_____

_____

In your opinion, do you have to demonstrate obedience to your spouse?

_____
_____
_____
_____
_____

Do you have to demonstrate obedience to your family? _____

_____
_____
_____
_____

What about being obedience to your children? _____

_____
_____
_____
_____

Who are you taking counsels from? _____

_____
_____
_____
_____

Do you think that disobedience cause someone to experience tribulations? _____

_____
_____
_____
_____

Can you cite an incident where you were disobedient? _____

_____
_____
_____
_____

What does disobedient look like? _____

_____
_____

_____

_____

What was the consequence that you suffer for being disobedient? ___

_____

_____

_____

_____

Overcoming Challenges of Life

Quotation: *Life challenges are set-ups for mindset changes. Changing minds healing nations by Gurmay Effrige Fraser*

The people who inflicted pain in my life are the same people who promised to love me and protect me, but instead, I became fearful and untrusting of them. When I came to America at the age of sixteen, I never felt welcomed by my brother and sister, my siblings. My brother and sister would harass me as often as possible. My brother would eat all the food, even though he knew that others did not eat. He would change the television channel if he came into the house and met other people watching television. While my sister would spit in my food and bully me into doing her laundry and her chores or else, she pushed herself into my physical space and physically threatened me to say what she would do to me if I didn't comply. My sister threatened to beat my unborn baby, my daughter, out of my body. Of course, when I brought this to my parents' attention, our mother indicated that I was older than her and I should want peace between us. Funny, I was not the one creating havoc and was made to accept and tolerate these abuses.

Even when I reported to my mother with proof that my sister stole my financial information and went to the bank, she forged my signature and withdrew my money. I was calling the police to press charges for theft, but my mother said that if I pressed charges, there would be nobody to take care of my sister's child. By the way, my sister never apologized nor repaid this money, nor has she replaced the belongings that she stole. My sister stole my new clothing and gave them to her friend and her friend's sister. Even my shoes she stole and gave them away, and what she did not give away, she took scissors and cut my clothing into a threat. Whenever I received my paycheck and tax return refunds, I always hid them on my body because she stole my money repeatedly.

I realized that for my mental stability and the safety of my unborn baby, I had to remove herself and find my own space. Also, I would never allow my daughter to be a victim after she was born by staying in my family's apartment while my mentally deranged sister was still living there. I did not trust anyone to raise my children but me. When my first child was born, my sister became very jealous. My sister would steal my baby supplies, including her food, pampers, cream, and milk, and use them for her first son.

Does any of the following below pertain to you or someone?

How do you describe challenges? _____
_____
_____
_____
_____

When you first experience a challenge what were your thoughts? ___
_____
_____
_____
_____

What are some of the challenges that you have experienced in your life?
_____
_____
_____
_____
_____

What did you learn from those challenges? _____
_____
_____
_____
_____

Do you feel that the lessons you've learnt from those challenges helped you to make wiser decisions? _____

_____

_____

_____

How long did it take you to learn from those challenges? _____

_____

_____

_____

Did you reap the benefits from those challenges? _____

_____

_____

_____

Who have you inspired from those lessons that you've learned? _____

_____

_____

_____

Do you feel that they were people that you needed to forgive? _____

_____

_____

_____

Have you forgiven those who wrong you? _____

_____

_____

_____

Did you feel that you needed to forgive yourself? _____

_____

_____

_____

Why is forgiveness important to you? _____

_____

_____

_____

_____

How does forgiveness affect your journey in life? _____

_____

_____

_____

_____

How are you inspired now when faced with a challenge? _____

_____

_____

_____

_____

Do you feel that your challenges pushed you to discover your true self and purpose? _____

_____

_____

_____

_____

Did you ever envision that those challenges would be resolve? _____

_____

_____

_____

_____

What state of mind did you envision that you would be in now? _____

_____

_____

_____

_____

Did life challenges made you bitter, angry, blameful, resourceful, empowered? _____

_____

_____

_____

_____

What advice do you have for anyone that is going through challenges?

_____

_____

_____

_____

_____

Do you think that each person has challenges to go through? _____

_____

_____

_____

_____

Do you recall whether Jesus Christ, our Lord and Savior had challenges to go through? _____

_____

_____

_____

_____

Do you use your challenges to blame, judge, persecute, teach, bless, deliver, guide, mentor? _____

_____

_____

_____

_____

Do you know what your spiritual gifts are? _____

_____

_____

_____

_____

Do you feel by understanding your challenges you would get to know your spiritual gifts? _____

_____

_____

_____

_____

What plans do you have in pursuing your spiritual gifts? _____

_____

_____

_____

_____

Do you know in what capacity do you plan to pursue your spiritual gifts? _____

_____

_____

_____

_____

When Enough Is Enough?

Quotation: *When you stop taking authority over your life, you then give someone else permission to take authority by Gurmay Effrige Fraser*

Looking back over my life, I began to stand on my authority to prevent abuse in my personal and professional life. I refused to settle in any relationship where there was any abuse. I also now had my children who saw me as their role model, and I was never going to compromise my safety or my children. I was not going to agree against the things I stood up against to prevent and risk my life to say that I have a marriage while living a life of fear and secret because of the abuse and abusive conditions.

I understand that this life is all I have, and I will not compromise because of ignorance or not studying God's Word on relationships, family, finances, etc. I understand that my children would do precisely what they see me do. Therefore, I continue to thrive on being a positive role model in my children's lives and the lives of other people that God has assigned to me. I no longer remain silent. Things that are abusive because silence is an agreement or no longer do I come into any agreement with any person or system that has any indication or connotation of abuse. I had many struggles to overcome in my marriage.

Effective communication was a challenge. When my then-husband, Conroy, and I were together, he was accustomed to refuse not to speak to me for weeks or using profanity when he spoke to me. I told him that his intentional silence or abusive behaviors were no longer tolerated, and I held him accountable for his behavior in our relationship. I modeled how Conroy would speak to me, and I clearly stated what I would not tolerate and what I would not accept.

On one occasion, I refused to be physically intimate with Conroy because not only did he refuse to speak to me, but he would also not answer his phone when I called him. On another occasion, I refused to become physically intimate with Conroy, which made him so angry. I physically fought Conroy and asked him to get off me, which made him angry. Conroy left the bedroom. He returned and walked toward me, and I thought that he was going to the master bathroom, but instead, he turned toward me, and he climbed on top of me, and pinned my shoulder down with his hand while he held a butcher knife to my chest with the tip of the knife that I felt on my skin. I grabbed the house phone to call 911, and he knocked it out of my hand; he told me that he would kill me the next time I called 911. He then raped me, and then he rolled off me.

I was so traumatized that I was shaking and ran into the closet with a pillow and blanket to sleep on the floor. Then God spoke to me and told me to get off the floor and return to the bed. I then went and got Conroy's mother, staying with us for the summer, to babysit his children. She was in the guest room, and I brought her to our master bedroom. I told her what happened, and her response to me was that I should know better and not to worry about Conroy because he did not mean to do what he did by putting a knife on my chest to where I felt the tip of the knife on the skin of my chest. Conroy's mother also said that one day Conroy's ex-wife called her and said she was afraid of him because he threatened to kill her over some discord. Funny, his mother was unaware that Conroy mentioned that same incident to me. He said that after he and his ex-wife were married. They argued, and he was angry with her. Later that night, while she was in bed, he was still up and cleaning his gun in the dark. His ex-wife was shot by him when she snuck up on him, and he thought that it was a robber. I then asked him how he cleaned his gun in the dark and would not hear if someone was breaking into his house especially if you are up and awake. I was nervous after he told me that, and I was also afraid not to get him upset because his recall of the shooting caused me to become afraid of him. After I got my thoughts together, I told him that his mother had got to leave my home because she was enabling his abusive behaviors. HE TESTED ME when I told Conroy that he was no longer allowed to abuse me.

Conroy continued his infidelity and made hotel arrangements for December 31st. To January 1st. 2008 in Florida with his lover. He requested me to babysit his twin daughters, who I was helping him raise. He told me he had a job interview in Florida for those dates as a truck driver. I did some research about the company that he claimed he would be interviewed at. I told him that he could most certainly go on his interview on these legal holidays, but he was also taking his children because I was not their babysitter. He went and took his children with him to Virginia at his sister's home to be babysat. And that was the last time his children were in my home, praise God.

When he returned from his vacation, I discussed the unpaid bills. However, he had a bad attitude and proceeded to pick a fight. During that period, even though I provided money toward the bills as I always did, he paid none but took my money. All the bills in my home were not paid, including the mortgage that was now in foreclosure. He responded that I did not deserve to be in the home; instead, I should be homeless and on the street. I then told him that I was not allowing any leaches, like him, Conroy around me and that he needed to pack and leave.

I reminded Conroy that I hired him to work at my company as a driver, and when he got the job, he had to use my expedition because his car was in the shop. I gave him money to take it out because he had nothing, not a pot to pee in or a window to throw the pee out. He began packing by throwing all my belongings from the master bedroom. I reminded him that I was staying and he needed to remove his things because he was leaving my home. I reminded him that he had moved into my home in Brooklyn and the house in Georgia I bought, and my home in North Carolina I bought, and as I reflected now, I realized that he never had any money or resources but talk and lots of ideas that never materialized into anything. He then proceeded and hit me with his shoulders and stated, "I hit you, so now you hit me back, and I will show you what I will do to you." He called me stupid, a stupid b.... He stated that he only married me to get his green card. I told him he was the stupid b.... because he had his green card many years ago, so why was he still here in my home. I told him that was fine because the God I serve would judge between the two of us that day, and God would decide who would remain in my home. The court evicted him with a restraining order because my life was in imminent danger, and I remained in my home to this day.

He returned to my home unannounced, but I denied him access; he sent me text messages begging me to be friends with him, but I never did. Conroy is remarried for the third time now, but he continued to call me and leave messages, he texts me in sexual languages, and I had to block Conroy from my social media platforms and phone. I told Conroy that I did not qualify him to be a friend of mine or to come into my space or my environment. One day in April 2016, he showed up at my home in North Carolina demanding that he needed to talk with me; he kept banging on my door, and 911 was called. Conroy evaded being served with court papers and a restraining order to keep him away from me, and he continued to run and hide.

Accountability

What does accountability mean to you? _____
_____
_____
_____
_____

How are you accountable for your life? _____
_____
_____
_____
_____

Do you have an accountability plan? _____
_____
_____
_____
_____

What steps do you take to ensure that you are fully accountable for you?
_____
_____
_____

_____

_____

Do you think that your spiritual life needs to be held accountable?

_____

_____

_____

_____

What is your plan for spiritual accountability? _____

_____

_____

_____

What is your assignment? (Not your decision but your discovery) ___

_____

_____

_____

What things do you hate? (Assigned to correct) _____

_____

_____

_____

What are some of the things that grieve your spirit? (Call to heal) ___

_____

_____

_____

What do you love to do? (Your skills, passion, gifts & wisdom) _____

_____

_____

_____

How are you preparing for your assignment? _____

_____

_____

_____

_____

What two (2) words can you use to describe yourself? _____

_____

_____

_____

_____

Have you or are you in a season of isolation? _____

_____

_____

_____

_____

Have you or do you feel that you're in a season of waiting? _____

_____

_____

_____

_____

What problem do you have or experienced that frustrates you? (God assigned you to solve) _____

_____

_____

_____

_____

Have you ever-experienced spiritual restoration? _____

_____

_____

_____

_____

What has spiritual restoration been for you? _____

_____

_____

_____

_____

What is your journey to spiritual restoration? _____

_____

_____

_____

_____

What are you doing to prevent abuse to you and your loved ones? ____

_____

_____

_____

_____

Do rejection, forgiveness; obedience and love travel the road to spiritual
restoration? _____

_____

_____

_____

_____

Do your children see you as their role model? _____

_____

_____

_____

_____

Have you ever been in a situation that you felt unsafe? _____

_____

_____

_____

_____

Did you fear you would be injured? _____

_____

_____

_____

_____

What happened? _____

_____

_____

_____

_____

Do you think that it is your responsibility to care for your generation?

_____

_____

_____

_____

_____

What can you do to make a better life for your generation? _____

_____

_____

_____

_____

Are you your brothers' keeper? _____

_____

_____

_____

_____

How do you demonstrate that you are your brothers' keeper? _____

_____

_____

_____

_____

Are you silent about abuse in your community? _____

_____

_____

_____

_____

What have you done to stop and prevent abuse? _____

_____

_____

_____

What things are important to you in your relationships? _____

_____

_____

_____

_____

What things are important to you your marriage? _____
_____
_____
_____
_____

What things are important in your relationship with your children?
_____
_____
_____
_____
_____

How about the relationship at work? _____
_____
_____
_____

How would you describe your relationship at church? _____
_____
_____
_____

Are you fellowshipping at the right church? _____
_____
_____
_____

How did you come to that decision to be at that location? _____
_____
_____
_____

As you reflect on your spiritual life, would you say that it is elevated or not? _____

_____

_____

_____

_____

What did you have enough of in your life and will no longer tolerate?

_____

_____

_____

_____

_____

What wise counsel do you have to share with others? _____

_____

_____

_____

Why do you feel that each person should be accountable for his/her life?

_____

_____

_____

_____

_____

What might happen if someone chooses to relinquish the power to think for himself or herself? _____

_____

_____

_____

_____

How do you feel to be able to think and decide for yourself? _____

_____

_____

_____

_____

As a man thinketh in his heart so, is he? What does this mean to you?

_____

_____

_____

_____

_____

Not Who You Are But Who You Become

Quotation: *Worst thing in life is to wait for it to happen instead of you make it happen by Gurmay Effrige Fraser*

I want to share something with you, and what I would like to share with you is to ask you: Who are you? Who are you? Who are you? Who do you think you are? We define ourselves by how society defines us. We see ourselves by how our families see us. So, when I ask you, who *are you?* You cannot answer because you don't know who you are. When we respond, we define who we are by saying that we are a doctor, a teacher, a pastor's wives, a mother, a homemaker, etc. We define who we are by how our environment defines us. I am here to talk to the other you that is within you, whose you are.

Listen, life at times throws us all kinds of curve balls. At three months of age, I was poisoned by a cousin who did not like me because of my skin color. I was abused sexually and molested. I was sick for many years. I suffered academically and socially and had many behavioral problems. I want to tell you something -- at a young age, I decided that I had to take the authority over my life and fight for my life, and I also realized that every day of my life would be a fight. I had to determine who I am, and you must decide who you are, so let's go through the journey.

Who are you? Who are you? You have hidden seeds of greatness within you, which needs to be planted in good soil. You are going to go through struggles in life. Many people look at life as the harbor. Sometimes we want to be comfortable. We go to college as society tells us, get a good education, get a good job, get married, buy a house, and think that is life. This is not life because it does not determine who

185

you are but because you have seeds of greatness within you. Until you begin to commit and walk in your true potential, you will never know who you are.

Many of us have faced many challenges in the life of abuse, marital issues, drugs, death in the family, hospitalization, relationship issues, etc. When I was getting my master's degree, I was always angry and ambitious, and I realized that I had to take care of my own life. I couldn't leave that responsibility to my parents or anyone else. I always had to go the extra mile. During those times, I lost the two best friends of my life -- two siblings. The police murdered my brother in his own home. My sister had some pain, was diagnosed with an ectopic pregnancy, and died in the hospital in less than a week. I became furious and began to drink to ease the pain. But I stopped myself and said that the things that I would not tolerate in my life, I would not allow. Because as a single parent with two young children, I realized that I did not want my children to be abused, and sometimes as parents, when life affairs begin to cause us stress, we begin to use drugs or other things to calm the pain. As a result, we might end up abusing our children. So, I'm telling you to look at your life critically, look at your life from your heart, and you're going to begin to determine who you are. Who are you?

You are fantastic, and you are powerful, you are unstoppable, and you can choose because life itself is a journey. It's not what happens to us in life; what happens to us in life is what defines us. I want to leave this thought with you, who you are, switch from who you are, and become who God says you are. By faith, I decided to change my situation because I understood that God needed me to repent by changing my mind about who God says I am. God needs me to get things on earth that He has stored in Heaven. God needs my body, my temple, for His spirit to live. God gave us all authority and power. Whatsoever I bind on earth, God bounds in Heaven; and what I lose on earth, God loses in Heaven. The gospel of the Kingdom states that God is restoring us to our place of dominion authority on earth, as He is restoring us as He promises according to His purpose in the book of John. "And if we know that He hears us, whatever we ask, we know that we have the petitions that we have asked of Him." (1John 5:15). I continue to understand that I am an Ambassador of God and was sent here on earth to have dominion, rule, and lead as I am reunited and restored to God's Kingdom, my heritage. I am from the Kingdom of God, and I am under Heaven's Kingdom and I am wealthy according to God's Kingdom. God is obligated to supply all of my needs because I am a King, and He is the King over me, King of Kings. I can attest to this: God is truly putting me back to my dominion authority on earth, and everything He had placed in me before the foundations when He formed me and knew me had been restored in my journey to spiritual restoration.

This is a lifestyle inventory of yourself:

How would you describe your attitude, behavior, mood, feelings, lifestyle, decisions, etc.? _____

_____
_____
_____
_____

What do you like to do? _____

_____
_____
_____
_____

What don't you like to do? _____

_____
_____
_____
_____

What are you passionate about? _____

_____
_____
_____
_____

What can you do well? _____

_____
_____

_____

_____

Do you prefer to work alone? _____

_____

_____

_____

_____

Do you like working as part of a team? _____

_____

_____

_____

_____

Can you set and keep your own schedule? _____

_____

_____

_____

_____

Are you able to see things differently and process and complete these things? _____

_____

_____

_____

_____

Do you have to be told, reminded, supervised closely to start, follow through and to complete assignments? _____

_____

_____

_____

_____

What are your study habits? _____

_____

_____

_____

_____

What is your work habit at work and at home? _____

_____

_____

_____

_____

Are you dependable? _____

_____

_____

_____

_____

If you are unable to complete assignments, how do you let your superiors know? _____

_____

_____

_____

_____

Do you become overwhelmed at assignments or projects? _____

_____

_____

_____

_____

Can you break complex problems into small workable pieces? _____

_____

_____

_____

_____

Do you like to be around people more than fifty (50) percent of the time? _____

_____

_____

_____

_____

Do you like being with yourself more than fifty (50) percent of the time?

_____

_____

_____

_____

_____

What are your strengths? _____

_____

_____

_____

_____

What are your skills? _____

_____

_____

_____

_____

What are some of the things that you enjoyed doing at work? _____

_____

_____

_____

_____

What are your favorite subjects in school/college? _____

_____

_____

_____

_____

Do you like to use your hands? _____

_____

_____

_____

_____

Do you like to read? _____

_____

_____

Do you enjoy writing? _____

What about taking notes? _____

Do you like to figure things out? _____

Do you like to use office machines, like calculators, fax, printers, computers, telephone, etc.? _____

Do you know who you are? _____

Do you like to give counsel? _____

Do people ask you for advice? _____

_____

_____

_____

Do you get angry/frustrated when people don't follow your advice?

_____

_____

_____

_____

_____

Who do you think you are? _____

_____

_____

_____

How do you see yourself? _____

_____

_____

_____

How do you define yourself? _____

_____

_____

_____

How do you take your authority? _____

_____

_____

_____

You must determine who you are? _____

_____

_____

_____

What are your seeds of greatness? _____

_____

_____

_____

_____

What do you believe is your destiny? _____

_____

_____

_____

_____

What commitments are you making to walk in your destiny? _____

_____

_____

_____

_____

What are your true potentials? _____

_____

_____

_____

_____

How do you hold yourself responsibility for walking in your destiny?

_____

_____

_____

_____

_____

Do you think that your tribulations were for you? _____

_____

_____

_____

_____

What advise do you have to share to help someone to walk in his or
her destiny? _____

_____

_____

_____

_____

What are you asking and believing God for? _____

_____

_____

_____

_____

Do you know that God wants to prosper you? _____

_____

_____

_____

_____

Understanding God's Kingdom Principles

Because God showed me visions and dreams and allowed me to endure trials and tribulations, and I began to seek Him and His righteousness, I became empowered under these persecutions I endured. I began to love and pray for people, even enemies, and forgive people who did me wrong. I began to also pray for my forgiveness and release my enemies, known and unknown. I then received the fruit of the Spirit: love, peace, joy, longsuffering, patience, kindness, and goodness.

The pressures and stresses of the persecutions of single parenting, abuses, divorce, major surgeries, accidents, abandonment, financial lack, and limitations caused my horizons to become so expand into graduation from colleges, caring for and educating my children, starting several businesses, developing websites, online and offline businesses, best seller author, empowerment speaker – and these things caused me to become connected to great people I did not know. God said in His Word that our major gift would make room for us, but our minor gifts will establish us. What a Big God I serve. God sent me a great family of God, my wonderful, blessed children, who at times also endured my trials and tribulations to whom I will forever be indebted. To God is the glory. God continues to transform me, and God is now supplying all my needs according to His riches in glory, and according to God's Word, He said that no good thing would He withhold from those that walk upright. I thrive to daily walk upright, and though it is challenging, especially when challenges show up, I must remind myself that God is with me, and He continues to provide for all my children's needs and my needs.

God's purpose for us is to rule and to rule over our flesh, not to be ruled, and not to rule over each other, but we're responsible for mastering, governing, managing, and controlling the earth's resources. When we walk short of who God says we are, we open ourselves to medical, physical, and mental illnesses and problems. We are all created as rulers and kings. As it is listed in the KJV of the Bible, "Then shall the King say unto them on his right hand, Come, ye blessed of my Father, inherit the kingdom prepared for you from the foundation of the world:" (Matthew 25:34).

The Kingdom of God suffers violence, and the violent must take back the Kingdom of God by force. The Kingdom of God does not come because we show up at church gatherings and stand and watch and feel that because it is not happening to us, we don't need to open our mouths. Silence is agreement. If something bad happens to one of us, it also happens to all of us. God created Adam only, and we all came from Adam. Therefore, everything that we need is already in us. However, we each must make sacrifices to study the Word of God to show ourselves approved and to get understanding as we apply the Word of God for our lives, our family, our work environment, and every place that our feet tread when God sends us as He moves in us and has His being in us.

What is God's purpose for us? God's purpose for us is to dominate the earth and all its resources and steward them, as is stated in the book of Genesis. According to the KJV, God said, "And God said, Let us make man in our image, after our likeness: and let them have dominion over the fish of the sea, and over the fowl of the air, and over the cattle, and over all the earth, and over every creeping thing that creepeth upon the earth. So God created man in his own image, in the image of God created he him; male and female created he them." (Genesis 1: 26-27). God is Spirit, and when He speaks, His Word is the law even unto Himself, and He can't violate His Word or principle.

Our Kingdom dominion for our lives as stated in the KJV of the Bible:" The Lord shall increase you more and more, you and your children. Ye are blessed of the Lord which made heaven and earth. The heaven, even the heavens, are the Lord's: but the earth hath he given to the children of men" (Psalm 115: 14-16).

God is not pleased by our tears, pain, or mourning and complaining. God is pleased by our faith in Him, for without faith, it is impossible to please God. In His Word, in the KJV of the Bible, it reads, "But without faith it is impossible to please him: for he that cometh to God must believe that he is, and that he is a rewarder of them that diligently seek him" (Hebrews 11:6). God's Word is a law unto Himself, written in the Bible in the KJV, "God is not a man, that he should lie; neither the son of man, that he should repent: hath he said, and shall he not do it? or hath he spoken, and shall he not make it good? Behold, I have received commandment to bless: and he hath blessed; and I cannot reverse it" (Numbers 23:19-20).

We must begin to understand that God wants us to be blessed in health and wholeness, love, prosperity, wealth, finances, debt freedom, creativity, a great relationship, great stewardship of His resources, bless others that need blessings, and walk in our destiny according to His plans for our lives.

God does not want us to allow ourselves to be ruled over the desires of our flesh: pride, passion, greed, jealousy, selfishness, lust, abuse, drugs, loving money, power, liquor, adultery, possessions, limitations, financial debt, fear, doubts that often rule over us. We might ask why we shouldn't love money when we have bills to pay? Loving money exposes someone's heart and thoughts that might be corrupt; applying money to answer things is what's important. Sometimes I believe that we need to remember that money is not only about work but also about processing us to take our rightful position as leaders. It is this simple. We must learn to make money work for us because that is its function, and when we understand that, it will multiply itself a hundredfold and more.

The Bible writes, "And the multitude of them that believed were of one heart and of one soul: neither said any of them that ought of the things which he possessed was his own; but they had all things common. And with great power gave the apostles witness of the resurrection of the Lord Jesus: and great grace was upon them all. Neither was there any among them that lacked: for as many as were possessors of lands or houses sold them and brought the prices of the things that were sold, And laid them down at the apostles' feet: and distribution was made unto every man according as he had need" (Acts 4:32-35)? These people were now masters over their money; therefore, money did not dominate them. I know that people sometimes don't like me because as I understand who God says I am, I must remember to only speak words of life, health, prosperity, healing, deliverance, salvation, restoration, etc., over my life and other people's lives. I recalled hearing people say about me, "Who does she think she is?" I know who I am and who God says that I am. I usually ask them, "Do you know who you are?"

Walk in Who God Said that we are

God said in His Word in the KJV, But ye are a chosen generation, a royal priesthood, an holy nation, a peculiar people; that ye should shew forth the praises of him who hath called you out of darkness into his marvellous light; (1Peter 2:9). When I began to understand who I am in Jesus Christ and how God created me, my thoughts began to shift, and my belief also shifted. According to the Bible in the KJV, "So God created man in his own image, in the image of God created he him; male and female created he them" (Genesis 1:27). God creates us for awesome work, according to KJV in the Bible "For we are his workmanship, created in Christ Jesus unto good works, which God hath before ordained that we should walk in them" (Ephesians 2:10). Also, important that we are the seeds of Abraham. The Bible stated in KJV, "And if ye be Christ's, then are ye Abraham's seed, and heirs according to the promise" (Galatians 3:29).

What have you gone through or going through in your life journey?

How does God speak to you? _____

_____

_____

_____

_____

Do you get visions and dreams? _____

_____

_____

_____

_____

What do you think about those visions and dreams? _____

_____

_____

_____

_____

Would you say that you endure persecutions? _____

_____

_____

_____

Are you a better person due to the persecutions? _____

_____

_____

_____

Are you a bitter person because of the persecutions? _____

_____

_____

_____

How do you feel about the people that persecuted you? _____

_____

_____

_____

Do you have a relationship with people that persecuted you? _____

_____

_____

_____

How would you describe the relationship? _____

_____

_____

_____

Describe how the persecutions allowed you to grow in the things of God? _____

_____

_____

_____

_____

What violence have you suffered? _____

_____

_____

_____

_____

What are you doing about the violence? _____

_____

_____

_____

_____

Can you change something that you will not confront? _____

_____

_____

_____

_____

Have you taken your authority back by force? _____

_____

_____

_____

_____

What does God's Kingdom principles mean to you? _____

_____

_____

_____

What does in the beginning God created heaven and earth means to you? _____

_____

_____

_____

_____

How are you preparing your spiritual life? _____

_____

_____

_____

_____

What is God's purpose for you? (Genesis 1:26-27) _____

_____

_____

_____

_____

Do you think that someone's tears move God? _____

_____

_____

_____

_____

What does faith and believe means to you? _____

_____

_____

_____

_____

What does God is not a man, that He should lie, nor a son of man, that He should repent means? _____

_____

_____

_____

_____

What God has for me it is for me means to you? _____

_____

_____

_____

What does Matthew 6:33 means to you? _____

_____

_____

_____

_____

How are you obedient to God's mandate in Isaiah 61:1? _____
_____
_____
_____
_____

What do you do to love yourself? _____
_____
_____
_____
_____

How do you demonstrate God's command to love your neighbor as
you love yourself? _____
_____
_____
_____
_____

Do you think that someone can love his/her neighbor before him or
herself? _____
_____
_____
_____
_____

What changes are you going to make to be obedient to God's
commandment? _____
_____
_____
_____
_____

What does Matthew 6:12 means to you "and forgive us our debts, as
we also have forgiven our debtors." _____
_____
_____
_____
_____

What have you created from the gifts and talents that God gave you?
_____

_____
_____
_____
_____

Do you know that when we don't use our skills and talents that becomes a debt? _____
_____
_____
_____
_____

Do you need to ask God for forgiveness for not creating from those raw materials that God gave you? _____
_____
_____
_____
_____

When do you plan to start to create those things that only you have the BLUEPRINT to create? _____
_____
_____
_____
_____

What are your plans to forgive your debtors? _____
_____
_____
_____
_____

What are some of the things that God wants you to rule over? _____
_____
_____
_____

What does seed sowing means to you? _____
_____
_____

_____

_____

Do you enjoy sowing seeds? _____

_____

_____

_____

_____

What does burnt offering means? _____

_____

_____

_____

_____

Is there a difference between the offering that Cain brought to God versus the offering Abel brought to God?

_____

_____

_____

_____

_____

What does "God hated Esau but love Jacob" means to you? _____

_____

_____

_____

_____

Living The Greatest Years Ever – I'm Here Now

After I was baptized and confessed that Jesus died for my sins and that He was raised from the dead after three days, I received the Holy Spirit. I was restored to my place of my Kingdom Authority and am learning God's purpose for me as I continue to have dominion on the earth and over all its resources. My life now is hopeful and peaceful, full of joy and happiness, and I am excited to wake up each day as I rise with expectancy and the power to conquer, inspire, empower, and encourage others. I am happy and now enjoy my life. I am an entrepreneur of multiple businesses and a best-selling author. I thank God for His grace and mercies.

I am healed, and Holy Spirit-filled; sickness, disease, and pain are far from me. I have no lack because all my needs are met. I am successful over daily challenges and living a victorious and prosperous life because I have a relationship with God, and He is now first in my life. His Holy Spirit now lives in me; He leads, guides, directs, and empowers me. It is awesome. I give my best and expect the best. I do not allow people who speak negatively about their lives to speak the same over mine, my children, my family, friends, or associates. I teach people about the confession of their lives, what God says they can have and can be, and who they are in Christ.

On December 7th. 2008 The Holy Spirit whispered to me, *arise up for your light has come.* The Holy Spirit continued by singing, *Holy is the lamb, the precious Lamb of God*; and finally, He said, *we fall, and we get up.* The King James Version of the Bible reads.

"Arise, shine; for thy light is come, and the glory of the Lord rises upon thee" (Isaiah 60:1).

God put something in me before He formed me in Giver, my mother's womb. He made me in the correct time and season according to His plan for my life because He knew that then I would agree with the challenges and tests of my life. God is the Author and Finisher of my faith; even though I endured the trials and tribulations, these situations were necessary to ignite and purify God's anointing in my life.

The Kingdom of God in me had to be released to set the captives free. God knew that I could handle these assignments because His Holy Spirit is in me, and God does it through me. Once I repented by changing my mind, and I began to have the mind of God, God then began to work His plan to restore me to my rightful place in my journey to spiritual restoration. As an Ambassador of the Kingdom of God, I understand that I do not have to accept pain, abuse, suffering, mediocrity, poverty, and trouble.

God desires to restore us to our Kingdom position to take dominion and authority over the birds, fish, and earthly realm – and even over the things that were once perceived to have authority over me and us. I continue to seek a daily relationship with Our Heavenly Father. As a Kingdom citizen, I am victorious by the power of the Spirit of God that resides in me, the anointing of God upon my life as I boldly journey toward God's Perfect Will, destiny, and plans for my life.

I live a life of fasting. As part of my lifestyle, I frequently study and read many books to acquire an understanding of Jesus, my big brother -- as I understand that I am included in God's Kingdom, and my big brother is Jesus. I continue to surround myself with the Kingdom of God and God's Kingdom principles. I am aligned with a corporate body of faithful believers, and our church family is shepherded by an anointed vessel of God. I continue to teach the Kingdom of God principles and provided classes, workshops, and community involvement to his congregation. I am blessed to have parents and family who taught me how to endure. I am doubly blessed to have children who are truly blessings of God. I was ordained on 2/19/2011 as a Prophetess, and I am an intercessor and began my ministry named God Spell Prophetic Ministries, Inc. Theme: Midnight Cry.

Changing Minds Healing Nations

This book, My Journey to Spiritual Restoration, ordained by God before the foundation, would have been a real challenge to complete at this time without the love and support of my Abba Father, Daddy. In addition, my children and my spiritual family. God has given me the title of this book with the book's last word first. As I continue to put God's interests first and represent Him faithfully, He will care for me, my children, spiritual and biological family, friends, and associates. In His word, He said that once I seek Him first and His righteousness, He will give me the desires of my heart.

I was the seed that God has spoken before the foundations, and His seed shall not return to Him void. I shall accomplish everything that God has placed in me. My tribulations, abuse, and trials were not for me. God was only using me because of His assignment and anointing in and on my life. Remember, a tree can't taste its fruit. I thirsted for wisdom and to know what God's Word says about His Kingdom principles and lifestyle, marriage, relationships, parenting, finances...

I desire to learn God's wisdom daily to discern the differences in time, season, and situations. God stepped into my tribulations and brought His order, and I continued to glorify Him. Righteous living comes from suffering in trying to do the right thing. God allowed people and things to leave my life for Him to bring the right people and things into my life according to His plan and perfect will for my life. Finally, I said, "God, it is not my will but God's will; let God's perfect Kingdom come through me and let His perfect will be done on earth, in me, as it is in Heaven." I am living and walking in destiny; for my light is come, and the glory of the Lord rises upon me.

On December 5th. 2008 at 2:36 PM, on vacation with a friend at Myrtle Beach, South Carolina, my cellular phone rang, and the number on my caller identification read 777-777-7777. My friend and I looked at the number, then I answered my phone, but there was no response, and no one answered. I turned to my friend and said that God had just called to inform me that He is with me always, and I am blessed and highly favored by God and man and woman. We called that number several times after but there was no answer. Shortly afterward, the Holy

Spirit whispered to me, "See, I give you the vision." The Holy Spirit continued to speak, saying, "In the beginning was the Word, and now the Word is life." I am not here to process; I merely would like to say to us that to God is the glory.

Also, on 12/07/08, God whispered, "I have completed the works I've begun in all of us." I pray in the Name of Jesus that the holy Angels of God surround us, and the presence of God engulfs us. I speak like a King, and I pray as a Priest. Arise and Shine, I'm here now and will not be moved, for the glory of God is upon my life., my children, our families, friends, associates, and loved ones. To God is the glory.

My prayer for us is Lord God. In the matchless name of Jesus Christ of Nazareth, I stand in the gap and agreement with my children, biologically and spiritually, family, friends, and associates around the four corners of the earth where this book is destined to travel. I decree and declare that no weapon shall fashion, form or prosper in or over our lives, our health, our body, our mind, our soul, our spirit, our finances, our marriages, our homes, businesses, job, education, the works of our hands and all that God has placed and attached to our lives, shall prosper. I speak to principalities, their cohorts, and they shall not affect our lives, and I bind every work from the root of darkness, generational curses, strongholds, transgressions, iniquities, regions of captivity, sickness, diseases, stagnation, stoppage, blockages, delays, denials, and cast them out and now make you become a part of the footstool of Jesus, in Jesus' Name. I decree and declare in Jesus' name that their tactics, strategies, plots, and plans for our lives are canceled and are now rendered null and void. For the weapons of our warfare are not carnal but mighty in God in the pulling down of strongholds and the casting down of vain imagination and every high thing that exalts itself above the nature of God. In Jesus' Name, I command the release of God's Kingdom alternatives and spitiual inheritances for our lives and everyone God has placed in our lives. I release the blessings of Abraham, Isaac, Jacob, Joseph, and the Wisdom of Solomon and Jesus in Jesus' name in and over our lives. I release an abundance of fresh deposits of God's anointing, prosperity, debt freedom, wealth, health, healing, extended health, whole life, godly relationships, the gift of His Holy Spirit, and the fruits of the Holy Spirit into our lives.

I agree with herself and the Holy Spirit in me, and I command our holy Angels of God to be released in, on, and over our lives and wherever the Lord of the Harvest sends this book. I seal this prayer and all future warfare prayers in the name of Jesus, the Word of God, and the blood of Jesus, Amen.

Your Reflections and Assessments on the questions below:

Do you feel that God used your trials, tribulations and situations to prepare you for life? _____

_____

_____

_____

_____

Why do you feel that way? _____

_____

_____

_____

Do you blame God for your challenges in life? _____

_____

_____

_____

What are good ways that God used your tribulations to prepare you?

_____

_____

_____

_____

How would you describe your life then compare to now? _____

_____

_____

_____

Name some of the great life lessons that you have learnt _____

_____

_____

_____

_____

How do you feel about your lessons? _____

_____

_____

_____

Are you equipped to teach, speak, and mentor someone that might be going through what you went through? _____

_____

_____

_____

What advice would you give to a protégé? _____

_____

_____

_____

Do you believe that it is important to be a protégé? _____

_____

_____

_____

Do you feel it is important to be a mentor? _____

_____

_____

_____

How do you know that God's hand is upon your life for good? _____

_____

_____

_____

Where do you think you would have ended up if God did not direct your steps? _____

_____

_____

_____

How do you feel about your life now? _____

_____

_____

_____

Do you think that your life has been a journey? _____

_____

_____

_____

Is/was your life a harbor? _____

_____

_____

_____

Is it dangerous for your life to become a harbor? _____

_____

_____

_____

Can God place fresh wine in old wine skin? _____

_____

_____

_____

What advice do you have for someone that is still complaining about the bad hand that life has dealt him/her? _____

_____

_____

_____

_____

Do you blame your abusers? _____

_____

_____

_____

_____

Do you believe that you are stronger now because of the abuse? ____

_____

_____

_____

_____

What is your word of wise counsel to anyone that wants to be pity?

_____

_____

_____

_____

Do you see any positive changes in your life? _____

_____

_____

_____

_____

How has your life change? _____

_____

_____

_____

Do you have a testimony? _____

_____

_____

_____

How have you overcome by the word of your testimony? _____

_____

_____

_____

_____

Do you believe that God choose you? _____

_____

_____

_____

Do you believe that you are living your greatest years now? _____

_____

_____

_____

What advice do you have for someone that is blaming someone for his/her circumstances? _____

_____

_____

_____

Does your life resemble the life of the man by the pool of Bethesda John 5:2-9 for 38 years? _____

_____

_____

_____

Some people think that their pastor will change their condition, what do you think? _____

_____

_____

_____

Others are waiting, what do you think these people are waiting for?

_____

_____

_____

_____

_____

What advice you have for people that are waiting? _____

_____

_____

_____

_____

Are you waiting for someone to do what God has called you to do?

_____

_____

_____

_____

_____

Do you think waiting resolves anything? _____

_____

_____

_____

_____

Can you share your best lessons from your preparation of issues?

_____

_____

_____

_____

_____

Now do you know your purpose? _____

_____

_____

_____

_____

Do you think that most people have the courage to stand up for
unrighteous behaviors? _____

_____

_____

_____

_____

Do you blame them for not standing up? _____

_____

_____

_____

_____

Do you know that silence is agreement? _____

_____

_____

_____

_____

How will you inspire someone that is not bold enough to stand up for what's right? _____

_____

_____

_____

_____

Where do you go from here? _____

_____

_____

_____

_____